Nomasomali

NOMASOMALI

UBOMI BAM

MARJORIE NOMASOMALI
GONIWE NKOMO

REAL AFRICAN PUBLISHERS

Published by Real African Publishers
PO Box 3317
Houghton
Johannesburg 2041

www.realafricanpublishers.com

First published in February 2021

© Marjorie Nomasomali Goniwe Nkomo

ISBN 978-1-928341-85-7

Editor: Angela McClelland
Production editor: Reedwaan Vally
Cover design: Adam Rumball
Cover painting: Sally Rumball

I dedicate this book to
the women of South Africa,
especially *ooMama basezilaleni*,
for whom freedom's promise remains elusive

and

to my grandchildren, whom I love dearly,
and all the children of South Africa.
I pray that for you, the future is so much brighter.

Contents

Foreword

This book by Mama Nomasomali Marjorie Goniwe Nkomo is a long-awaited addition to a rare literature that depicts lived African experiences of the twentieth century that have long since been wiped away from the media, school textbooks and the general public space. The author shares complex stories of her upbringing and the joys of being part of a large community where everyone lends a hand towards a better life.

The book tackles the subject of human tragedies and successes in an uncompromising manner, beyond customary polarised tendencies aimed at self-pity. It presents us with strong women who fought and triumphed against all odds of the unforgiving history of South Africa. The writing in this book signals that the author is beyond tendencies towards self-aggrandisation and hubris. Mama Nomasomali humbly tells the stories of unsung heroines and their plight as forgotten freedom fighters. She writes of their selfless courage and questions why they today live in squalor along with the people they sought to liberate. The writing is forceful without being vulgar and graceful without being apologetic.

The diverse experiences and multiple temporalities traversed by Mama Nomasomali make her the most suitable conduit to convey a message of tomorrow to the Girl Child in Africa. It is a story and a lesson of the unforgiving era on how to overcome triple oppression as a Black citizen, Black woman and Black professional, including the demands of a patriarchal society.

The purpose of this book is to tell, without self-pity, a story of ordinary grandmothers, mothers and daughters who, forced by circumstances, become unsung heroines of the struggle against apartheid. Stories in the book cut through veils of formality and niceties of political correctness to sing praise to the courage of an altruistic mother, daughter, wife, friend and neighbour. The writing permeates through all layers of difficulty to finally deliver a message that no matter how desperate and gloomy a situation may seem, perseverance always pays.

However, the book is by no measure a rags to riches narrative or the usual motivational dream-woven magic. Instead, the writing systematically unpacks the thinking and rationale behind every success that the author and people around her achieve. Mama Nomasomali guides the reader through a labyrinth of life endured by those around her without any exaggeration. She shares the ups and downs of a journey taken by a young Black South African towards professional success in a world that is dead set on cancelling her efforts.

The book takes a bold turn in pointing out that the past may have been better because at least families held together through thick and thin in fighting a recognisable enemy. It continues to point out that current freedoms have invaded and turned upside down the last bastion of traditions and culture: the morals and ethics of an African family.

The book uses everyday occurrences and moments of an African Black home to describe the workings of *ubuntu*. Mama Nomasomali describes the language, the art of storytelling and traditions of nuclear and extended family as repositories of an African ethical moment and collective memory. Mama attributes her own success and that of others in society to the resilience of *ubuntu* in her community.

In the sincerest and almost naked manner, Mama Nomasomali paints a society where men are absent fathers, brothers, uncles, providers and protectors of community. The only males present in her community are young boys cared for by grandmothers, mothers and sisters until they are ready to join their fathers in the cities for a pittance. It is a story where men only return home ridden with diseases to be nursed into their early graves.

The book draws our awareness to the foundational role of family, both nuclear and extended, as a platform for shaping future generations, fighting adversity and rejoicing in small and big victories. In not so many words, the book poses a pertinent question that has gained traction in the present social unrest: 'When is the liberation of the Black masses going to take place?'

Mama Nomasomali laments the present appalling degenerate state of her childhood village before boldly reminding everyone that the present South Africa owes its existence and prosperity to the sacrifice of unsung heroines and heroes of the struggle against apartheid.

If anything is to be taken from this book, it is the courage to fight the ever-present pervasive attempts of an invisible thumb that aims to oppress the female body in a free South Africa. The book summons all South Africans to revisit original childhood lessons where the roadmap of *ubuntu* is still very much alive in African folklore, where it took an entire village to raise a child.

The author reminds me of my grandmother, who would repeatedly caution her grandchildren: '*Lalelani abazali benu kukhona nizokhula nibe ngabantu abaqotho.*' Roughly translated, that means: 'Listen to your parents so that you may grow to become decent members of the community.' Those words are etched on my brain and help me find a way home to a community whose lessons guide all of my practice to this day.

Professor Paul Zilungisele TEMBE
Thabo Mbeki African School of Public and International Affairs (TM School)
University of South Africa
September 2020

Acknowledgements

There are so many people to whom I am grateful for shaping my life and inspiring me across my life's journey: *Ndiyabulela.*

My late mother, Maryjane Malusana Sakhile Goniwe: *Umama.* Nyathi to some and MaNyathi to others. Small in stature, you were a great pillar of support for us, your children and, later, your grandchildren. We lost *Tata* so early in our lives, and you were mother and father to us. You farmed to keep us fed, rooted our lives in the Church and devised creative ways of moulding us. Your graphic renditions, through storytelling, instilled a deep sense of justice in us and successfully kept us from misdemeanour.

My late father, Lenford Goniwe: *Tata*, you were not there as I grew up, but the idea of you was a constant presence. I know now that people do not die as long as they and their deeds are still remembered – because that was true of you. Around us, as we grew up, people spoke of you, your ubuntu and your great love of education. The community assisted in making sure that the children of the village, including your own, were educated, as that was your undying wish.

The late Rutherford Goniwe, my grandfather, who was always remembered as a great documenter for the community: one of those adept practitioners of the craft of oral tradition, and my late grandmother, Martha Goniwe, who was a warm, loving woman.

My late sister, Lindiwe Goniwe, fondly known as Guda, how can I forget you, sister dearest? You paid for my tuition at Ohlange High School. I thank you greatly.

Mbulelo, my dear and now late brother, I miss the competition that we had over our mother's love. It was good while it lasted, but then you took the trophy when you became a priest of the Methodist Church, the Reverend Mbulelo Goniwe!

There is my birth family, the Goniwe family, and my marriage family, the Nkomo family. All beloved, all fellow travellers on this journey. I joined the Nkomo family when I married Abraham Sokhaya Nkomo. My dear husband, Abe Sokhaya, I have travelled this rugged road with you, I the Goniwe girl from *elalini lase maMpondweni*, moved to a Pretoria township, Atteridgeville, *ePheli*. Along our journey I have learnt that the mystery of love is that it does not run out, it is a never ending stream. The more you give of it, there more of it there is to give. Abe, my husband we have seen it all. We have done it all and we are still a strong enduring unit. Hold on my dearest and do not tire!

Dr. William Fredrick Nkomo, *Doda*, as you were lovingly called, for me, you were the world in one person. You united nations, you revered education, and you taught by example: first as a teacher and then principal. Later, you left teaching to become a doctor, the first doctor in our community. The Methodist Church was your anchor as you raised your children in a world where they had lost their mother at an early age. You were always gathering people together, and inspiring them came so naturally to you, *Umany'izizwe Doda*. I learnt to love you and will never forget the joy and colour you brought with you – always.

Your children became my sisters and brother: Portia, Connie, Koko and Kali. What a road we were to travel together.

Your brothers and sisters – all special, all loved – how they each touched the world and left it a better place. Aunt Pricilla and her family, Uncle Gideon, Aunt Glory and Uncle Peter: I know you sit with them now, proudly looking at what you began.

To you, my dear children: Susan Nokunyamezela, Nolitha Naledi, Phakamile William Frederick, Gcobani Phumelele, Woyisile Bulelani, Marumo Lubabalo, God blessed me with you; it has not been easy due to our involvement in the myriad activities that became part of our lives. On some days, I was not available when you would have wanted me to be with you, but we did find each other in our hearts. Thank you for having given me the purpose of being a mother. I value you and will always keep you close to my heart.

My *makotis*: named here by their given names and the names I and my sisters gave to them – their *amagama asekhaya*. Grace Byron, who is now Grace Nolufefe, married to Woyisile Nkomo and mother to Gabriella and Kaia. Severine, who is now Severine NoRainbow, married to Phakamile and mother to Pierre Manyizizwe. Ringelani Ndlovu is now Ringe Sange, married to Marumo and mother to Zenzele. Those are the mothers of four of my grandchildren. My son Gcobani is a single parent and father of Nosipho. Life presents itself in many forms. Who could have imagined that we could be so varied and so warm with each other? Look at the rainbow nation that we have become.

I also thank Anna Tsotetsi – Magogo – my friend, sister and comrade. Aluta Continua. I remember you always.

Rose Lawrence, friend and fellow traveller on this long and tenuous journey. You were there through the King Edward days and the early Pretoria days, and now we are *gogos* together.

Thank you all.

The profession of author comes at such a late stage. For that reason, I am grateful to have found so much support and encouragement from so many. Special thanks goes to Nana Mthimkhulu of NanaStory Arts and Education for her encouragement during the early stages of my writing.

And finally, to Angela McClelland. Thank you, *Sisi*, I trusted you with my precious creation, a gift for my grandchildren, and you helped nurture it with such care. You saw my vision and helped me bring it forward. *Ndiyabulela.*

In closing, I am struck by the words of Albertina Sisulu as cited by Elinor Sisulu in *In Our Lifetime*:

> We are each required to walk our own road and then stop, assess what we have learnt and share it with others. It is only in this way that the next generation can learn from those who came before them, so that they can take the journey forward when we can no longer continue. We can do no more than tell them our story, it is then up to them to make of it what they will.

Introduction

I was born on 16 November 1941 in Bizana in the Eastern Cape, a place then known as the Transkei, part of the Cape Colony. South Africa was still a union then and would remain so until 1961 when it became a republic of the select under the apartheid regime.

The South Africa I grew up in was very different from the South Africa we live in now. I know there is still much to be done to build the 'new South Africa' that we dreamed of, but I am proud of the role that I, generations of my family and so many others I knew, know and love, played in bringing us towards the momentous events of 27 April 1994.

Segregation, later legislated as apartheid, took up many decades of our history in South Africa. Segregation, as we experienced it, meant more than the imposed separation of groups. In addition to keeping groups separate along ethnic, racial, religious and sometimes even gender lines, subjugation was both endemic and normalised.

When I grew up in Bizana, most households looked like ours. They were households headed by women. Even though I knew that the men from those homes – fathers and adult brothers – were still alive, they were constantly away at the mines. All homesteads were effectively run by women; agricultural production was sustained by women; where there was livestock, it was managed by women, and children were raised, fed and educated by women. In time, the boys would grow, and most of them would end up at The Employent Bureau of Africa (TEBA) offices where they would be signed off to the mines, almost as if they were commodities. Most girls would grow up, become mothers, and the cycle would continue: young girls raising boys, most of whom they would be compelled to deliver to the mines and the city, at their prime, to serve the capitalist beast that would discard them when they became old and sick. The women (their mothers, aunts, sisters and daughters) those young men had left behind at the time of their prime would once again have to care for them when they returned: sick, infirm or dying.

So, I grew up aware that women were the engine powering the community and the economy. But that engine never got serviced, and it was continuously, inexorably deteriorating. The lie we had been fed was that our communities and homes required the remittances the men would earn from the mines or white farms so we could survive. The reality was that, increasingly, the mines and white farmers and the new emerging white urban households required cheap African labour to be viable. As a result of that outward flow of labour and the lack of input the other way around, African women were effectively subsidising both capital and apartheid. Poverty was growing. Everyone left Bizana.

I was aware that the only way out of poverty was education. The work my elder siblings had done in maintaining the homestead with Mama, and Sis' Guda paying for my education, meant that I had some freedom to pursue a career within the limits that my family could afford.

The career I chose was nursing, for which I would study at King Edward VIII in Durban. Nursing had the advantage of allowing me to earn a stipend while studying. Even better: many of the young girls I was friends with, and whom I had met at Ohlange, were also headed there.

King Edward, in those days, was a world of its own. The training we underwent to become nurses was gruelling and comprehensive. As immersed as we were in the training – and it was intense – we were also aware of the many shifts around us. South Africa had become a republic, and apartheid repression was at its height. It was also the time of Black Consciousness. Stephen Bantu Biko was rallying African professionals, in particular, doctors, to serve African communities in places where there were none. On campuses and all across the country, political mobilisation was taking place.

At King Edward VIII, I met a young medical student, Abraham Sokhaya Nkomo, and when we decided to get married, the Mzaidumes were there. Looking back, it seems that they have always been there for me at significant times.

When I spent a year in Johannesburg, I stayed with them, as my Aunt Nontombi (*Dadobawo*) had married into that family.

Back when I attended secondary school at Saint Lewis Betrand's in Newcastle, I went with my cousin But'Lindwa Mzaidume, who was a teacher there. He was the son of *Dadobawo* uNontombi Mda. When Abe told his father of our intention to get married, it was Uncle Lewellen Mzaidume (who was married to Phyllis Mzaidume, Aunt Nontombi's mother-in-law) whom my father-in-law (*Doda*) approached to assist him in the negotiations with Mama and the Goniwes.

Once the negotiations were complete, the two of us were free to proceed with the official marriage registration. In those days, if one were to get married, especially if not from Natal, it was considered wise to ensure that you did so anywhere *but* Natal. Young professional couples like ourselves considered marriages entered into in Natal totally repressive to women and thought that those marriages infantilised women, making them perpetual minors. In the other provinces (Transvaal, Orange Free State and the Cape), even though women entering into marriage remained minors until 1984, the conditions of women in those marriages were considered preferable to those of women who entered into marriage in Natal. The collusion between the apartheid brand of patriarchy and Zulu chauvinism had, in our opinion, resulted in a toxic outcome for women.

Abe and I thus made a conscious decision to get married in uMzimkhulu, which, in those days, was part of the Cape Colony. Marriage dispensation in the Cape was more favourable to us because of its proximity: uMzimkhulu was easily accessible for those of us studying in Natal who wanted to be married under a different dispensation.

Now to fill in the details.

Part 1

Before

KwaNdunge, the *lali* (village) where I was born, was named after its traditional leader, *Nkosi* (King) Ndunge. *Nkosi* Ndunge, who was at the throne in KwaNdunge when I was growing up, was a colourful figure whom we children enjoyed watching as he went about the village. We were amused by the spectacle of him walking along the path, followed by an entourage of praise singers (*iimbongi*) and *iinduna* (headmen) acclaiming the king and exalting his 'great' deeds and those of his ancestors. As children, we would follow behind, much like the children following the Pied Piper of Hamelin. On occasion, *Nkosi* Ndunge would visit the school, perhaps seeking an audience. The teachers probably welcomed that reprieve from their endless tasks, as they would let the king address us. That was always an enjoyable interlude, and to this day, I remember *Nkosi* Ndunge's loud, booming voice shouting, '*Ndiphethe aphe; Kuphethe mina apha* (I rule here; it is I who rules here).'

A *lali* consists of a collection of homesteads, each of which had one main building, often of a Western style with a large verandah, like ours was, and a number of huts built around or next to it that were either rectangular or circular in shape. The circular ones are called *rondavels*; they are built with mud bricks and roofed with thatch made of twigs and grass. The roof is domed and is in the shape of an inverted cone. The exterior is whitewashed with lime from the eaves down to the midpoint, which is then finished off with a coat of mud plaster from that point to the floor. Viewed from a distance, it is a beautiful sight. The homesteads are well-spaced from each other, providing numerous open places for children to play, well within the sight of the adults.

My homestead was bordered by trees that formed a semicircle or arc in the main part of the property. Next to the homestead were several acres of land that had been set aside for cultivation. Mostly, we cultivated mealies but also had a smaller field where we grew potatoes, sweet potatoes, tomatoes, onions, spinach and other crops for household consumption.

From the vantage point of the main house, one got the impression that the land extended endlessly in one direction, as far as the eye could see.

Everyone in Ndunge knew that when my father died, *Nkosi* Ndunge had tried to take the land away from Mama. However, MaNyathi would have none of that, and she took *iNkosi* to the magistrate where she represented herself, arguing that she would not be able to care for her children (six of them) without the land. Where would she go with them? I do not know what the magistrate said, but the outcome was that Mama kept the land. In contrast, in a traditional court, Mama would not have been able to represent herself, as women are not allowed to be heard there. In fact, up to this day, women have fought against that, and women from all provinces where there are communities living in rural areas have opposed the Traditional Authorities Bill.

The homestead to the south of our home belonged to the principal of the local primary school. The *rondavels* on his property were built with cement bricks and finished with a light-yellow lime. They had corrugated iron roofs. That was a beautiful homestead. Having a home built with cement and brick walls was considered very prestigious. Our neighbour to the north was the brother of the principal, and he too was a teacher.

I remember the village always with the eye of a child. I recall the vast spaces of open land between the homesteads and the road, which were, on occasion, used for grazing. That was before the overcrowding that bedevils Ndunge today. I remember the majesty of the Engeli Mountains, the range of which extends along the western horizon of Ndunge. Those are the mountains referred to by Tat'uOliver Tambo in the books *Beyond the Engeli Mountains* by Luli Callinicos and *OR Tambo – Teacher, Lawyer and Freedom Fighter* by Gladstone Sandi Baai.

What I recall about our homestead is that, apart from the main kitchen with the coal stove in the main Western-style house, there was a *rondavel* behind that main house that was used as a kitchen. On the floor in the centre of that hut there was a circular formation about three feet in diameter and slightly elevated at the periphery. That was the hearth, the heart of our home. Practically, it was used as a place where family meals were cooked. In reality, it was so much more: it was the place where the family gathered together every evening to share stories about what had happened during the day. After that, supper would be served, the dishes cleared, and then prayers would follow before everyone retired for the night.

Those were wonderful times. I am grateful that the feared phrase, *Ikati ilal'eziko*, did not apply to our homestead. *Ikati ilal'eziko* means that the cat sleeps in the hearth. A cool hearth in a homestead indicates hunger in that home: an idle hearth where food is never cooked. In that sense, the idiom bespeaks the fact that a hearth that has not been used for cooking becomes a comfortable place for a cat to snuggle in. The hearth was the centre of family activities, and on cold Eastern Cape evenings, we would sit around it on grass mats (*amacantsi*).

One of my recollections of growing up *elalini* (in the village) is making cups and cups of tea. The adults, it seemed, were addicted to it. If they did not have any, they would complain of having a headache that could only be remedied by tea. In the morning, before they had done anything, many of the adults would have had two cups of tea. We used loose tea leaves, and our tea was made in a teapot that would sit on hot ashes until the brew was nice and strong. When the tea was ready, we would use a strainer to catch the leaves when pouring it into cups. Making tea was a skill. It is easier these days with electric kettles and teabags: place one teabag into one cup and fill with the boiled water from the kettle: such convenience.

I have found the love of tea to be something that brings people, especially women, together. As children, we traded stories about our common quest to escape the task of making tea. And that, I have found, was not limited to Amampondweni, where I grew up. There are many stories across the country about attempts to escape chores – even among those generations born after ourselves, when we were the adults demanding cups of the brew.

For example, many, many years later, I was to hear Mmemogolo Semane, Queen Mother of the Bafokeng people, tell the story of Fossie, her son, and his now famous tea incident. As Mmemogolo Semane told it, Fossie, who was six at the time and ever the charmer, had offered to brew his mother a cup of tea. As she was busy with household chores, that offer was quite welcome. So, Fossie went off on his errand to make the tea and returned carrying a cupful for his eager mother. Somehow, while handing it to her, the cup tipped over and quite a lot of tea spilt onto her. Once the gasps and shock had subsided, Fossie exclaimed with great satisfaction, 'You know, Mme, I helped you! I helped you!' And noticing his mother's puzzled look, he explained, 'The water was not boiling; I did not boil the water, Mama.' Fossie had used warm water from the tap to make his mother's tea.

As I recall, when it came to tea, the brand was king – or maybe I should say, queen. My mother's favourite tea brand was Five Roses. If one was sent to the village to buy tea and returned with a different brand, there would be 'war' at home. Some people would add different flavours to their cup of tea: perhaps a pinch of salt or fresh red pepper. My mother flavoured her tea with peppermint drops. She used a particular brand of peppermint extract from Lennon industries. Those *druppels* could be purchased over the counter and had a peppermint flavour.

Adults would concoct stories intended to ensure that they always got their tea. For example, to gain our eagerness to supply her with endless cups of it, Mama diagnosed herself as having a heart problem, (*isifo se ntliziyo*). She announced that Five Roses tea was good for her because, she insisted, it contained less tannin than the other available brands.

A good cup of tea had to be enjoyed with milk, preferably warmed milk. On days when there was no milk at home, one of us would be sent with a mug to ask for some from the neighbours. That would be reciprocated when they did not have milk and came, cup in hand, to ask us for some. Milk was short, mostly, when the calves had met the cows before the milking was done.

⌘

Names have a special significance for my people. Among the Sotho, there is a proverb that says '*Leina ke seromo*', which means 'Your name is your fate or your purpose'. Even though it is the prerogative of the parents to name their newborn baby, they often do so in consultation with the elders of the family. With the Nguni people, one can tell the gender of a person by the prefix before their name. The prefix 'No' is usually attached to a girl's name. So, if a boy is named Themba, the female equivalent would be Nothemba or Nomathemba. Similarly, where a boy is named Sipho, a girl would be Nosipho or Nozipho.

Sometimes the elders would suggest the name of a deceased member of the family, hence recycling the name and, they hoped, the distinctive beloved traits of that person. Sometimes babies were given names that commemorated important events in the family or community. As mentioned, my name is Nomasomali, which commemorates the joy at the time of the Second World War when the Allied Forces were turned back in Somaliland and they returned home. That was a war we had nothing to do with; however, many men from our communities had been sent there, effectively as cannon fodder.

To follow the progress of loved ones during the War, the elders of the village used to go to the local magistrate's office (*ekantolo*) to hear about their fate as they advanced northwards across unknown lands. My paternal grandfather, Rutherford Goniwe, was among those elders. I am told that I was born on the very day Grandfather Rutherford came home from *ekantolo* with the glad news that the Allied troops had let the sons of Ndunge go, and they were on their way back home. They had been released in Somaliland. That was November 1941, and the War had ended for the sons of Ndunge. On arrival home, my grandfather was greeted with the further good news of the birth of his granddaughter, who was me.

Grandfather Rutherford promptly named me Nomasomali. I am told that, now and then, he would look at me, beaming with the biggest smile, and say '*E–Somali, basihlehlisile e–Somali*', meaning 'In Somaliland, they let us go; they released us in Somaliland'. I love my name; how can I not love it? Also, I do not know anyone else who has it. I am the only Nomasomali in the whole world, and that gladdens my heart.

The unfortunate thing is that, in those days, we were forced to have two names. In addition to our given name, and here I mean the *real* name given to a child, we were also required to have a 'first' name, which had to be an English name and was considered to be one's official name. We referred to that 'first' name as *igama las'ecaweni nase'skolweni*, (the Christian and school name).

Since the first name was to be used at church and school, it had to be one that Europeans would find easy to pronounce, thus the requirement for it to be an English name. That name was used for religious purposes such as baptismal and confirmation ceremonies, as the ministers of religion were white. Even though at primary school one's given name could be accommodated by the African teachers, a provision had to be made in case the child managed to get to the higher classes where an English name was required.

As a result, my beloved name, given to me by my Tat'oMkhulu, had to be dropped from all official documents and replaced with a name that should have been my second name.

When I was growing up, most parents were not familiar with many English names and were not bothered to come up with English names for their children. To assist officialdom, teachers often drew up lists of English names – randomly selected, purposeless names – for parents to choose from. My sister, Sis'Guda, who was the teacher of the beginners' class, had drawn up two such lists to make it easier for parents when they needed to select a name: one with girls' names and another with boys' names.

っ

In those days, I recall that it seemed to me that Ndunge was the world in itself. Expectations about what one could achieve or become were muted and, for the most part, children were not expected to pursue an education beyond Standard 5 or 6. By then, they would be educated enough to obtain employment as clerks in offices of the gold or coal mines. Not many girls attended school, and those who did would become sufficiently literate to assist their family by reading and answering letters from far-away relatives. When I was in Standard 5, I had a classmate who was a very bright girl. She was so good in arithmetic that the whole class envied her. One year, she confided to me that she would not be returning to school at the end of the June holidays, as she would be joining one of her brothers who was working as a miner in Johannesburg. Indeed, she did not return, and the class lost a strong motivator.

Girls were expected to concentrate on housework, which included chores such as fetching water from the river, weeding the mealie fields, making *igewu*, collecting firewood and a host of other related domestic activities. Generally, the firewood would be collected over a few weeks and piled high in a conspicuous location so that it was immediately visible to everyone. That served as an announcement that the girl or girls of that family were hardworking. The other more practical reason was to make the wood easily accessible to everyone. Ideally, there would be enough wood in the stack to supply the family with fuel for several weeks.

The primary responsibility of a good home was considered to be the production of marriageable girls. Girls were expected to display warmth, kindness, generosity and be sociable towards visitors, as it was believed that those attributes would serve them well in marriage.

One of the important skills for girls was to know the properties and uses of the plants that grew around the area. Girls would sometimes be required to pick wild spinach from the fields, which was a special skill because one had to be able to distinguish between the edible plants and the poisonous ones. Every time we harvested wild spinach and greens, my mother would carefully inspect them before cooking to remove any poisonous plants that might have been accidentally picked. After a thunderstorm, mushrooms would appear overnight in the veld, but only the adults were allowed to harvest them. Even then, there were occasions where one who was experienced in picking mushrooms would make a mistake, and the whole family would be wiped out. In addition, we were seriously warned by the adults who told us that there were certain mushrooms that could make whomever ate them go mad.

Generally, the eating of mushrooms was discouraged, especially if one did not know their source. On one occasion, when Mama visited us in Pretoria, I, having undergone various culinary classes at prestigious establishments there, offered to serve her a fancy mushroom dish, which was my signature dish at the time. Yo, did she give me a suspicious look. She was not going to touch it! I tried to reassure her that the mushrooms I was offering her were not poisonous. After which she answered that she did not eat food that did not have seeds and said that she did not know that here in Pretoria we had mushroom seeds. She looked on as others ate and complimented my mushroom dish – but she did not touch it. So much for fine dining.

Marriages were normally negotiated between families. Forced marriages were very rare. Given the increase in financial difficulties facing families in my area, arranged marriages, whereby girls eloped, *ukuthwala*, became more and more common. *Ukuthwala* literally means to be carried away and refers to being taken to the home of the fiancé. The following morning, messengers would be sent to the girl's parents to report that the girl was now with them and that the family would not need to look for her. That was a formality. Custom then requires that a cow be sent to the girl's family to start the negotiations for *lobola* (dowry).

The practice of *ukuthwala* evolved among my people to accommodate families who, for many reasons, would not be in a position to pay the *lobola* at the point of the marriage, as was the custom, but would negotiate and pay it upon mutually agreed terms. That practice became more widespread because of the rise in poverty, and particularly among families with a lot of sons. Families with large numbers of boys of marriageable age invariably found the social demands for getting them married to be too costly. In those circumstances, arrangements for the elopement would be made with the consent of the girl and her family.

Ukuthwala, as it was practised then, was a progressive intervention in response to the social conditions of the time. It enabled two people who knew each other and were of the same age to legitimate their union in a way that was accepted and facilitated by the community. It was a recognised marriage under customary law. It was nothing like the present perversion of the practice, where old men abduct girl children (who would not by any means be considered as consenting or of marriageable age) and violate them. What is even more perverse is that often the little girls abducted for that purpose are girls from a single parent – from a woman-headed home.

When I was growing up, marriage was an essential rite of passage in my community. It bestowed the ultimate status of respectability on both the woman and the man. For the woman, it also meant that she would have to leave her home to live among her in-laws. She would also assume a new name at her new home, given by her mother-in-law: *igama lasekhaya* (home name).

Within the community, as a sign of respect, married women were called by their clan name and the prefix 'Ma' would be added to it. My mother's clan name is Nyathi; she was therefore called MaNyathi by members of the community. The primary objective of that practice is to enable the offspring to be aware of their relatives and avoid incestuous marriages. And sexual abuse of children was considered taboo.

At my home, I grew up knowing that one never refers to their grandparents by name. That was unheard of. I am not sure if it ever occurred to me then that grannies even *had* names. We called our paternal grandmother *Makhulu was'emaTolweni* because she came from the amaTolo clan and stayed among those people. From time to time, *Makhulu was'emaTolweni* would come and visit for two or three days. When we were growing up, our favourite visitors by far were our grandmothers. That was because *o'Makhulu* told the best *iinstomi*. *Iintsomi* are fantastical Xhosa folktales with all kinds of magic and talking animals and menacing monsters called *o'zaigeba*.

Usually when a guest came, my siblings and I would be happy because we knew that at least one chicken would be slaughtered and everybody would enjoy a good meal. Another source of enjoyment for us when *o'Makhulu* visited was the variations their visit brought to our daily routines. For instance, when *Makhulu was'emaTolweni* visited, we had the additional task of chasing the dogs away from the hut before evening prayers. *Makhulu* had the belief that dogs swallowed prayers. She believed that if we prayed in the presence of the dogs, our prayers would not reach their intended destination.

Another welcome change to the routine of us young ones during *Makhulu's* visits was sleeping in the same hut with her. In Mpondomise fashion, *Makhulu* wore her dress, made out Sechwechwe material, over layers and layers of petticoats. On the topmost petticoat, over her waist, *Makhulu* would have a pouch, which she tied at the back like an apron. That is where she kept some money and a small container of Vicks ointment (Vicks has a strong eucalyptus smell and is generally used for chest and nose problems). In that pouch, *Makhulu* would also keep a packet of XXX mints, which are round flat sweets, usually held in a cylindrical packet. Each night, when I went to sleep in the same hut as her, *Makhulu* would take out one of those mints and give it to me to suck. She told me that it would soothe my chest and was good for my voice. Always, after giving me one of the mints, *Makhulu* would tell me not to tell the others because it was our secret. Later, we discovered that she did that with all of us at different times. In fact, we found out that she had the very same 'secret' with each one of us and had made each of us swear that we would not tell the others about it.

My maternal grandmother was *Makhulu wase'Mhlanga*, so-called because she came from a nearby *lali* called eMhlanga. From time to time, she too would come to visit us. One could just read from her face that *Makhulu was'eMhlanga* was a very unhappy woman. She did not have wrinkles as such, but her face was always gloomy, and she seldom laughed or smiled. Mama once told us that *Makhulu* had lived a difficult life. She told us that it was very difficult for her but did not elaborate any further. Questions about grownups and their ways were generally discouraged. In the case of *Makhulu wase'Mhlanga's* situation, that ban on questioning was not very helpful. It only served to leave us all the more curious about the very thing we were forbidden to ask questions about: *Makhulu* and her life. We wanted to know what was so difficult about it.

So, it was not surprising that this 'matter' and our questions regarding it occupied our thoughts all the time during *Makhulu's* visits to our home. During one of her visits, while we were gathered around listening to what she had to tell us, *Makhulu* caught me gazing at her. I had been unaware that I was literally staring – gawking at her! I had all kinds of questions in my mind and was wondering what those bad things were that Mama had implied had happened to her. Imagine my fright when I was shaken out of my thoughts by *Makhulu*. She wanted to know why I was staring at her. I grappled for an answer and blurted out the first thing that came to my mind. 'You are so beautiful, *Makhulu*,' I said. At that, everyone just burst out laughing. Even *Makhulu* laughed. She said, 'Yes, I know, my child. When I was a young girl, I was as beautiful as you are.' It is true: *Makhulu* was a very beautiful woman, but her face was very sad, especially when she had that faraway look, as if she did not see us right in front of her.

Some months later, I happened to be visiting *Makhulu* at her home in eMhlanga. I was going to stay with her for a while during my school holidays. On one of those days, *Makhulu* asked me to walk with her to the river to fetch water. So I did. Walking anywhere with *Makhulu* was fun. She always had interesting stories to tell. When we met with her friends, she would show off at my expense, telling them to look at how I had grown; to look at how beautiful I was Sometimes, in an attempt to show off how clever I was, she would ask me to recite a poem for them – any English poem I had learnt at school would do – and I would perform as requested:

One, two, three, four, five,
Once I caught a fish alive.
Six, seven, eight, nine, ten,
Then I let it go again.
Why did you let it go?
Because it bit my finger so.
Which finger did it bite?
This little finger on my right.

Anyway, on that occasion, as we were walking back from fetching the water, *Makhulu* and I had the path to ourselves. We were strolling along contentedly, balancing our pails of water on our heads. She was telling me something, so I was not really paying attention to our surroundings – I think because we were walking back home. I must have been concentrating on keeping my pail of water balanced on my head so as not to lose even a drop along the way. All of a sudden, there was a loud raucous noise, and a man on horseback rode towards us, shouting very loudly.

He stopped his horse right in front of us on the path. At that point, I was straining my neck, looking up at the man high up on the large horse. I noticed that he was holding the reins with one hand while pointing furiously at *Makhulu* with the second digit of his other hand. That man seemed so angry with *Makhulu*. He kept pointing at her, shouting obscenities and threatening to kill her. I had never seen or heard anyone scream or hurl insults at an adult before. I had never seen anyone talk disrespectfully to an elder person, much less scream at them. I was so frightened that I started crying.

Then the man got off the path and rode away in the opposite direction from where we were going, all the while, pointing and screaming. I was still crying and shaking with fright. *Makhulu* was quiet. After a while, I was able to speak. I asked *Makhulu* who that man was, and she told me that his name was Dingindawo, and she pointed at the direction of his homestead. That was all *Makhulu* said to me about it. I cannot remember much else about the rest of that day or night.

The following day, *Makhulu* was up very early, preparing my *mphako* 'provision' of chicken and *umbako* 'homemade bread'. She told me that some of the women from eMhlange would be travelling to my village later that morning and would accompany me home safely. They would also be carrying a message from *Makhulu* to my mother.

When I got home, I told everyone what had happened and begged my siblings to go back to Mhlanga with me because I was worried about the man, Dingindawo, who had said that he was going to kill our *makhulu*. However, Mama discouraged the expedition I was determined to embark upon and said that *Makhulu* would be alright and that we would pray for her. We prayed, but still I could not sleep because I kept seeing Dingindawo sticking out his finger, pointing and screaming at *Makhulu*. That happened every night until five days later when a messenger arrived from eMhlanga carrying a message from *Makhulu*. The messenger told Mama that *Makhulu's* thatched hut, the one that was used as a kitchen and had her hearth in it, had been torched the very night I had left the village with the ladies who had accompanied me home from eMhlanga. Luckily, no one had been injured. *Makhulu*, he said, was well. The elders were addressing the matter.

The messenger had brought with him a big live chicken which he said was for me from *Makhulu*, who was at that very moment busy working on the repairs to the hut. The messenger said that *Makhulu* wanted me to come back to Mhlanga and complete my interrupted visit and would send a message as soon as the repairs were finished.

When I asked Mama why *Makhulu's* hut had been torched, Mama's answer was vague, which was typical of adults at that time. She said that it was too complicated for her to explain. All that I needed to understand was that *Makhulu* had done nothing wrong. She said that we needed to give thanks that *Makhulu* had not been harmed. She also told me that *inkosi* at Mhlanga and the elders of the village had admonished Dingindawo. She said that the live chicken the messenger had brought was part of the compensation Dingindawo had to pay because he had shouted so disrespectfully at *Makhulu* and had made me cry. Mama was laughing as she told me that Dingindawo had been made to pay for the repairs to *Makhulu's* hut.

As I grew older, I became aware of the nasty, ugly practice of discrimination against the elderly, which is but one aspect of the scourge of women oppression. Widows, especially the older ones, who lived alone and were in good health and showed no sign of ailments, were always being accused of practising witchcraft. As a result, they could be subjected to untold harm, unless the elders or *iindunas* took charge to reverse the situation. Dingindawo's threat that he would kill *Makhulu* was not an empty one. The fact that *Makhulu* was known to have extensive knowledge of indigenous herbs, including their properties and uses, made her all the more vulnerable to the accusation of being a witch by people with nefarious intentions seeking outside explanations for their own ineptitude.

Many people from the various villages around Ndunge and Mhlanga knew *Makhulu wase'Mhlanga* and her vast expertise in the practice of traditional healing using herbs. That knowledge was very important in areas such as ours where the traditional healer would be the only one available for miles and miles. At home, Mama relied on *Makhulu was'eMhlanga* for all of our medical needs. *Makhulu* had also taken care of Mama and Mama's siblings' medical needs when they were growing up. So, when one of us came down with the flu, Mama would send a message to *Makhulu*, who would arrive the very same day carrying *ikhambi* and *umhlonyane* (fresh medicinal herbs that grew on the river bank).

Makhulu always stressed to us how important it was that the person working with medicinal plants, or any wild plants for that matter, was experienced and knowledgeable about the plants they were dealing with and all of their effects. She always had *ikhambi* and *umhlonyane* with her, as those were handy everyday remedies to her – like a Panado is to us here in the city. The difference was that one had to forage for *ikhambi* and *umhlonyane*. That is why Mama relied on *Makhulu* to get the herbs for us: she had the time and the expertise.

Ikhambi is a plant with leaves that look very much like those of the lemon verbena plant. The stalk is soft and juicy and has a strong bitter but somewhat soothing aftertaste. To treat flu symptoms, *ikhambi* would be pounded into a paste and mixed with water to form a deep green liquid. Mama would use that to soothe a sore throat. When I had a sore throat, Mama would wrap her index finger with a piece of lint. Then she would dip that finger into the liquid made of the pounded plant and rub my throat with it. It would be so painful at times that Mama did not avoid a bite or two. Generally, one needed only one application of that remedy, and then the throat was left to heal, which happened in a day or two.

Umhlonyane looks like grass with very small leaves. I knew that it was very good for bringing down a fever, easing a tight chest and healing upper respiratory infections. It would also be pounded and put into the three-legged pot that was placed on the fire to boil, uncovered. To my knowledge, medicinal herbs were never boiled with a lid on. What followed next was not popular with us children. The boiling pot would be removed from the fire and the sick child would be held over it by the mother. Mother, child and pot would be covered with a blanket, forming a steam tent. The child would kick, sweat and cry while the mother made sure that the pot didn't spill and burn the child. After that procedure, the child would be covered with a blanket to make sure that they were not exposed to the cold and then put to bed for the night.

Generally, most minor illnesses were dealt with at home using indigenous medicine. The challenge would arise when dealing with complications such as measles and bronchitis. At that time, there was one medical doctor serving Bizana and its surroundings, and he was in town, which was quite a distance from our village and difficult to reach. Because of that, many a child died on the way to the doctor. Even if one made it to the doctor's rooms, that was not a guarantee of survival. My favourite sister, sis'Nomvuzo, did not make it, in spite of having been taken to the village doctor.

Unlike *Makhulu wase'Mhlanga* and her peers, who explained illnesses and their prescribed cures to patients, those who consulted the doctor in Bizana were often left with very little understanding of the exact nature of an illness or the cause of a demise. They accepted the inevitable with resignation, referring to the scripture, 'The Lord giveth; the Lord taketh.'

Mothers who were compelled to take their children to the doctor had to demonstrate ultimate patience. They would arrive at the doctor's rooms and sit in a long line, waiting with anxious mothers from all of the other surrounding villages. When one's turn came to go in, the doctor would ask a few questions. He was always in a hurry and did not seem particularly attentive, so the mothers would provide monosyllabic answers, which seemed to be quite fine for the doctor. In part, that might have been due to language limitations on both sides.

According to the adults, every child was given the same medicine, even though the symptoms and ailments varied from one to the next. At the end of the consultation, the child would receive an injection (*isitofu*), and the mother would be given a pink liquid medicine and a packet of white tablets to administer to her child at home. There was never much in the way of an explanation. Those were the days before vaccinations and when clinics were rare commodities.

As for the grown-ups, going to see the town doctor when they were ill was a last resort. Only when the traditional doctor had said that they could no longer help the patient would one make the trip to the doctor in town. Once there, the doctor would examine the patient and, in all likelihood, refer them to a hospital. Most of the time, those who were seriously ill would be referred to hospitals in the neighbouring towns of Healdtown or Port Shepstone.

However, some patients were referred to hospitals as far away as Durban.

At the time, there were no ambulances, or they were not made available to us. Thus, it was the family's responsibility to arrange for the patient's transportation and the relative who would accompany them.

It didn't take long for word to get around the village that a member of the community was seriously ill and had been taken to the hospital. When the person who had accompanied them returned home, the community members would have already converged at the patient's house to be informed about their progress in hospital. The process of reporting to the community is an important one, and the word for it is *ukubika*, which literally translates as 'to announce'. The person who gives the report is referred to as *obikayo* (one who reports).

The *obikayo*, who is usually a relative, would then give a comprehensive account, beginning with the condition of the patient and details of when the patient and the accompanying relative had left the patient's home. The journey to the doctor in town and the condition of the patient during the journey would be described. There would be an account of the consultation with the doctor in the village, the referral to the hospital and the reaction of the patient to all of that. Then the name of the city in which the hospital the patient had been taken to would be provided. Every detail was shared: the means of transport used to reach the hospital; the length of time it took to get there; how the driver drove; the diagnosis provided by the hospital doctor, if any had been given, as well as the recommended intervention, which was yet to be transacted by the doctors.

For example, the person who had accompanied a patient might report that the doctor had said that the patient had a swollen small intestine (*uthunjana*) and would be operated on. The Xhosa term for operation is *ukuhlinza*, which translates as 'to slaughter' in English. The idea that someone would be operated on would therefore generate both fascination and fear. During the impromptu gathering of interested parties and neighbours, there would be an animated discussion about the presumed goings on in the operating theatre.

Those fantastical discussions would even include accounts about what the medical staff would be wearing in the theatre. There were always those who claimed to know such things, which seemed to give some reassurance to the family. For instance, if the discussion centred on the dress code of the medical staff, it might be reported that all those in the operating theatre would be dressed in white from head to toe and their faces covered with a white cloth, which left only their eyes and nose exposed.

Even the other doctors taking part in the procedure would be discussed and their jobs described. For example, it might be reported that there was also an anaesthetist in the operating room, who would most likely be described as 'a doctor who injects the patient so that they are asleep while all the cutting up takes place and sits next to the patient's head during the operation to monitor their breathing'. It would be said that, once the patient was asleep, 'the doctor puts the patient's soul in the luminous box that is positioned above the patient's head in the operating room. The anaesthetist doctor would then watch carefully to make sure that the patient's soul did not escape. The doctor never moves at all throughout the procedure because the patient is dependent on him to guide his soul back inside him at the end of the operation.'

Those discussions, based as they were on the accounts of those who had accompanied the patients and the inputs they had elicited from their audiences, were partly true, but they also had aspects of the fantastical, which was due in part to the paucity of factual information available to all parties. While their purpose was to demystify the hospital experience for the family and loved ones of the patient, those accounts also generated fear and anxiety that led to a general suspicion among the community of the Western biomedical health institutions and the 'dis-ease' they generated.

That was not helped by the fact that those who had to leave family members as patients in faraway hospitals often had to leave them there for long periods of time. Hospital visits were difficult under those circumstances, given the distances and costs involved. Sometimes, the family would find that the hospital stay had not been 'hospitable' for their loved ones. Sadly, in most cases, the family would have no means of ameliorating that situation for their loved ones.

Other times, a family would hear from the patient that the nurses, who were often the only people with access to them at the time, were complicit or even responsible for making their stay unbearable. In most situations, the patient would take advantage of the presence of loved ones and opt to discharge themselves and return home with them, no matter how severe their condition was. Nurses had such a bad reputation among my people then, and they continue to now.

Perhaps, in part, that is because nurses are at the bedside of the patient and thus available to them for a longer time than the rest of the medical team. Consequently, they bear the brunt of the patient's rage against the disregard and humiliation the patients experience in the 'ill health' system.

I have experienced the pain of watching loved ones being mistreated by the nurses on whom they are so dependent. Sadly, after two decades of freedom, my beloved Sisi'Guda was admitted to St Patrick's, a hospital that had not even existed when we were growing up. I was a nurse, and I cringed when I heard the pain in Sisi'Guda's voice as she described the ill-treatment she had received from the nurses at the hospital. The meanness and sheer pettiness. Imagine refusing to provide a patient with a blanket as she lies sick and shivering on a hospital stretcher during a frigid winter night in Bizana.

I experienced that again when my brother Mbulelo was admitted to the same hospital. On both occasions, we were forced to intervene, which entailed moving them out of the hospital. In the case of Sisi'Guda, that meant installing drips and the necessary equipment in our home and having her nieces and nephew, who fortunately are all qualified nurses, take care of her at home. I am glad that she spent what turned out to be her last days surrounded by those who loved her, her dignity intact. I remember the relief in her voice as she smiled and whispered loudly to my daughter, 'Suzi, oNursi ngo Satane, mtanami (Suzi, the nurses are Satans, my child).'

I am grateful that we could take Sisi out of there. I know that so many continue to suffer so much in what should be health care institutions. But I have gone way ahead of myself.

UMalume, one's mother's brother, is a significant figure in an African family. In my family, a family where there was no adult male, my uncle played the role of father in loco for my siblings and me. Once, I had to be taken to the doctor for a dental problem that required all of my milk teeth to be pulled out. Mama could not bring herself to take me, as she was afraid of having to watch the procedure. Because of that, Malume, as the resident co-parent, had to take me.

So, the two of us went. When it was my turn to go into the consultation room, I went in with Malume. He explained to the doctor what the problem was, whereupon I was told to sit on a stool in front of the doctor. Then I was told to open my mouth wide. He was not the kindest doctor. He picked up a menacing-looking instrument from a tray and came towards me, aiming it my mouth. As he was about to stick it in and pull out a tooth, Malume looked alarmed. He wanted to save me, so he stretched out his hand and shielded my mouth with it.

The doctor became very angry and stared venomously at Malume. Malume then apologised and told the doctor that he could continue. The doctor told *Malume* that it would be more useful if he were to use his hands to shield my eyes. The doctor told me again to open my mouth wide, which I did. My eyes were closed and *Malume* had his hand over them. The doctor proceeded to pull out nine teeth, one after the other, without any anesthesia. Under *nyamezela* (to endure), I simply had to persevere. Throughout that torment, *Malume* consoled me, saying '*Thula mtaka sisi, u Thixo ukhona*', which means 'Shush, child of my sister, do not cry. God is here'.

Malume worked as a shop assistant in a general dealer's store in the village. He never forgot our encounter with the 'dentist' and my courage in putting up with the ordeal. So, whenever he saw me pass his workplace, he would ask me to come in and would make me choose whatever I fancied from the deli section of the store. He would then take whatever I had selected to the person at the till and ask them to calculate the amount for him and write it in the book that recorded his debt (*isikweleti*) to be paid at the end of the month, when he would receive his salary.

Malume was so generous that I wondered whether he had anything left of his pay to take home at month-end. When I discussed that with my mother and my siblings, they agreed that I should avoid walking past *Malume's* workplace as much as I possibly could. They understood how difficult that would be, as there was only one long street where all of the shops in the town were situated. Therefore, we agreed that if I had to go to town, I would never walk on the side where *Malume's* shop was. Although that solved the problem, *Malume* became unhappy and complained that I was avoiding the shop.

꒰꒱

Living in a rural set-up has its hardships and challenges, which becomes evident if one has had the opportunity to live in a different setting. In rural life, it takes a long time to complete even the simplest household chores. As children growing up in that environment, we were aware of the steps each food product had to undergo before it could be consumed by humans. In contrast, I have heard it said, perhaps in jest, that children who grow up in urban areas believe that milk comes from a bottle.

For us, the different steps of food cultivation translated into different household chores, which were divided along gender lines. As girls, we would have to stamp the mealies and go to the river to collect water before going to school. Mother remained, preparing the family dinner.

Another chore that girls performed was cleaning the home. That, too, was very time consuming, as the floors of the huts were made of mud and were not cemented or tiled. To clean such a floor, one had to collect dung and use it to apply designs on the floor. It was also our task as girls to go to the village to buy, among other things, candles and paraffin for lighting at night. That entailed a long walk to the village and thus more time. Candles enabled us to do our homework once our household chores had been done. Doing homework and studying was difficult under those conditions because one was only allowed a short time to study at night for fear that the candles were used up faster the longer we kept them on. There was also the fear that a child might doze off while doing their homework, and the candle would topple and set fire. Despite that, doing schoolwork was not allowed while there was still light, since chores had to be done first.

Among my people, the birth of a child is a joyful event. For a young mother who is giving birth for the first time, it is an even more momentous occasion. Back in the day, the first child was usually born at the maternal home. Before the end of the nine-month gestation period, the expectant woman would travel to her parents' home to give birth. That would be the first and last time she would be nursed and taken care of by the elderly women in her family. During that time, information was shared among women about the care required by a newborn child, from the moment of its birth through the early stages of its development.

There were many shared myths among the women about practices that could make the process of giving birth easier. For instance, it was believed that the more active one is at the onset of labour, the shorter the labour will be. For that reason, at the onset of labour pains, a pregnant woman was encouraged to engage herself in various household chores as if nothing were happening.

For the most part, the community depended on a traditional midwife to assist; however, there was a limit to the extent of the assistance traditional midwives could provide when complications developed during labour. As a result, the infant mortality rate was quite high.

Generally, a woman who had given birth was expected to stay in the house for the first ten days afterwards.

The idiom *Isana elingakhali lifel'embelekweni* is commonly used among the Nguni-speaking people. Because the practice of carrying a baby on one's back is no longer as common as it used to be, that idiom requires some explanation. The Xhosa term used to refer to a newborn baby is *usana*. The verb, *ukufa*, means to die. *Ukubeleka* is the verb meaning to carry a baby on the back. The blanket used to carry a baby on one's back is *imbeleko*. *Ukukhala* means to cry. Thus, loosely translated, the idiom means that a baby that does not cry will die, unnoticed, on its mothers back. That is because a baby strapped to a person's back cannot be seen by the person carrying it. It is outside that person's range of vision; therefore, my people say that unless a baby tied to its mother's back announces its discomfort by crying when conditions become unbearable, it will die in that position.

The irony, of course, is that a child who is content will lie quietly on their mother's back while she does her chores in the house or field. But on occasion, disaster does occur. If, for example, it is a very hot day while the mother is hoeing in the fields, there is a strong possibility that the baby will swelter in the heat, become dehydrated and die.

Similarly, on a very cold day, the baby might be exposed to too much cold, become hypothermic and die. Should a child not cry while exposed to those harsh elements, the mother might mistakenly assume that all is fine with the baby.

♒

Traditionally, *imbizo* (a gathering or meeting) would be called by *inkosi* (the chief or king), who would call his tribe's men together to communicate or discuss matters of importance to the community. Traditionally, women did not participate in *iimbizo*.

A woman who was the head of a household would not be privy to the decisions made at *imbizo*. Therefore, to be informed of the outcomes of *imbizo*, such a woman would have to enquire about it from the men of the neighbouring homesteads, or her son, if she had one of an appropriate age.

Because women were not present when decisions were made in the community, if the matter being discussed in *imbizo* directly concerned them, they would have to be represented by men. That situation made the women vulnerable. For instance, as had been the case with Mama, when a man who is the head of a household passes away, *inkosi* could, at whim, dispossess the family of the deceased of their land. My mother experienced that misfortune when my father died. Mama had heard of that through those who had attended *imbizo*, and because she knew she could not appear and be heard among the elders, she had taken the only option she perceived as being open to her.

Mama had been so brave. Faced with the imminent threat of being dispossessed of the land she was cultivating to feed her children, she went to the village magistrate to plead her case. Mama was cunning as she appealed to that man by evoking my father as paterfamilias and her interests in continuing to uphold his duty of care for us as the basis for her holding on to the land. She argued that although her husband had died, his children still needed to be provided for. His children still needed to eat. She pointed out to the magistrate that the land *inkosi* was threatening to dispossess her of was her only means of sustaining her children. As a result of Mama's impassioned plea, the magistrate ordered that *inkosi* could not take the land away from her.

Although Mama had prevailed in her case, she did not escape the wrath of those who looked down on her for having defied *inkosi*. The issue of women's civil rights and their denial by traditional authorities remains fraught with tensions and contradictions to this day. In most cases, even though women work the land, in law, ownership and control of the land is vested with men.

In post-apartheid South Africa, in rural areas, including Bizana, more than 80 per cent of all households are headed by women. The government seems unperturbed about the conditions in which the mostly female inhabitants of those areas continue to subsist. It intends to disenfranchise women through enacting the highly contested Traditional Authority Bill, which, as Sizani Ngubane and members of the Rural Women's Movement have pointed out, would have women in rural areas falling outside the protection of the Constitution and made subject to the rule of the despotic traditional authorities in the areas in which they live. They would not have recourse to the option Mama took to protect her land from being taken by *inkosi*.

As a child growing up in a rural area, I remember Christmas time, and especially Christmas Day, very fondly. Mostly at that time, the men who had been away at the mines had returned, so some of the families were complete again. Parents did their best to make Christmas exciting for us children. We woke up very early in the morning to watch the sun dancing up in the sky.

Every effort would be made to ensure that the food that was served on

Christmas Day would be different from what we ate every other day. A sheep or a chicken would be slaughtered, and there would be other delights as well, like trifle. A trifle would be made without the luxury of a refrigerator but by positioning the jelly to set in a cool place. Once set, it would be decanted into a see-through dish lined with slices of Swiss roll and wedges of canned peach and then allowed to set further. Finally, a layer of cooled custard and a topping of whipped cream would be added. And sometimes, there would be rainbow sprinkles on top.

Usually, there would also be Christmas clothes for the children, which were always planned and prepared long before Christmas Day. For us girls, that was because the material for our dresses had to be bought and the dresses sewn at home by our mothers beforehand.

One year, several weeks before Christmas Day, Buti'Nyaniso, our elder brother who was a teacher, took my younger sister Vicks and me to the village to choose material for our Christmas dresses. Vicks chose a blue cloth, while I chose a green one. Although Mama had other chores to complete, she started with the dresses. First she would cut out the pattern and then begin to sew the dresses. Each time she had to stop sewing to do something else, she would fold both dresses into a bundle and put it inside the closed sewing machine. It seemed to us that those periods when the cloth was sitting untouched in the machine were numerous and inordinately long. So we started pestering her, begging her to please, please finish making our dresses. At last, she gave in and asked us to fetch the sewing machine and place it on the table so that she could proceed with the dresses. We did as she instructed and placed the sewing machine on the table. But then, just as Mama opened the lid of the machine, out jumped a big rat!

The three of us exchanged glances. We were very concerned. We knew that the rat must have done some damage. Each of us had a different wish. Mama's was that the rat had not done any damage to either of the dresses. Vicks's wish was that the blue dress had not been eaten, while I wished, 'Oh! Not the green dress!' Mama untied the bundle and, lo and behold, the green one had been damaged.

When Buti'Nyaniso was informed of that, he took pity on me and happily took me back to the shop to get material for another dress. Unfortunately, the green material was finished by then, and I had to choose a different one.

꒛

When I was growing up, the only religion that was recognised officially in the Transkei was Christianity. Therefore, in line with Christian precepts, no one was allowed to work on a Sunday. Children were taught to go to church on Sunday. Ploughing the fields or picking firewood was not allowed on a Sunday.

In keeping with the Third Commandment, 'Remember the Sabbath Day and keep it holy,' Sunday was observed by all the members of our community as a day of rest. No work was done on that day. That was the norm, even for those people who did not go to church. The only chore that was allowed was cooking the Sunday meal for family.

There were many myths that corroborated the notion that something bad would happen to anyone who did not abide by the Sabbath rule. For instance, we were told that if one were to look towards the moon on a clear night, one would see the outline of three forms. Those three forms were said to be a woman who went to pick up firewood from the forest on a Sunday; the second was a bundle of firewood, and the third form was said to be that of a dog – her dog that she had taken with her on her ill-fated mission. It was said that the woman who was trapped in the moon had defied the rule and gone to fetch firewood on a Sunday. On her way home, it is said, she was carried up by an unknown magnetic force, which defied gravity, and deposited in the moon.

It is also said that, as she was being lifted up – up towards the sky and into the moon – the bewildered, agitated woman uttered the following words: *ngeCawe*, *ngeCawe*, which means 'on Sunday, on Sunday'. We were awestricken, imagining that poor woman stuck in the moon, frozen there from generation to generation, in perpetuity.

Given the respect for the sanctity of Sunday that was instilled in us as children, it became very challenging for any person in the village who chose to deviate from it. I know a story about a man from our village called Tat'uSabelo. It is said that some time back, Tat'uSabelo had gone to work at the sugar plantations (*emobeni*) in Natal. At that time, it was common for men from our village to take a six-month contract to carry out seasonal work on the plantations in Natal.

Tat'uSabelo and his family were members of the Methodist Church and attended church services every Sunday with us in Ndunge. When he went to the sugar plantations, Tat'uSabelo left his family behind, but they continued to attend church with us. During his stay in Natal, Tat'uSabelo met with members of the Seventh Day Adventist Church who convinced him to join their faith. Members of that faith attend church on Saturdays. In our community, that faith was not known.

Before Sabelo returned home, he, as a newly converted member of the Seventh Day Adventist Church, started worshiping on Saturdays. He also commanded his wife, Manyawuza, to tell the members of our church that he and his family were now members of that new denomination.

Manyawuza, however, decided to ignore those instructions from Tat'uSabelo and continued coming to our church until her husband returned. When he did, he was determined to continue with his newfound religion. Accordingly, on the first Sunday after his return, Tat'uSabelo inspanned his oxen and went to plough his mealie field with Manyawuza in tow. Her role was to lead the cattle, walking in front, leading the way.

Walking thus on their way to the fields, they met with groups of congregants going to church. Those Christians were outraged to see such a blatant flouting of the precepts they held sacred. So, they stopped and shouted at Sabelo and Manyawuza, saying, 'What do you think you are doing? Do you want to join the woman in the moon?'

There was no answer from the couple. Instead, they walked even faster. People were late for the service watching the circus created by the couple who dared to do what was not done. According to Manyawuza, when they arrived at the gate of their mealie field, Tat'uSabelo had turned, looked at her and said, 'Manyawuza, *masigoduke ayikho lento*': 'Manyawuza, let us go home, this is just not on.'

The following Sunday, Tat'uSabelo and Manyawuza were the first people to arrive in church, and they never looked back to that denomination that Tat'uSabelo had sought to join.

The church, the family and the school formed a strong tripartite alliance in our community. It had been the missionaries who had established the schools in my village and the surrounding villages and, as a result, every school had a classroom that would be used for church services on Sundays. At my primary school, Ndunge Primary, the church services were conducted in the Standard 5 classroom. The school itself was a stone building. It was a solid structure that still stands today.

Each morning, the learners were required to assemble in the Standard 5 classroom to recite the Lord's Prayer, *Bawo wethu oseZulwini* (Our Father Who Art in Heaven). It was the role of the Standard 5 teacher to lead the school assembly.

The Standard 5 classroom was also the venue for all other community social events. During the Christmas period, the students who had returned home from their various boarding schools would conduct their Christmas socials in that same classroom cum church hall. The annual community concert would also be held there. At such a concert, various community members would showcase their talents, and there would be singing, entertaining skits and even dances.

Once every three months, the minister of our church, the Methodist Church of South Africa, would conduct the church service in our village. That would be a long service that included baptisms, the administration of Holy Communion and the distribution of membership tickets. The church services would start at eleven in the morning to accommodate those who had to travel long distances. As a rule, children were not allowed to sit in when Holy Communion was being administered, so we were always curious as to what the grown-ups were doing when they remained for Holy Communion. When we enquired about it, we were told that all would be revealed once we were confirmed as full members of the Methodist Church.

As children, we particularly enjoyed the part of the ceremony when we would be called to come forward and receive our membership tickets. That was exciting because the minister, who was a white man, would be calling out our names. The first names were not a problem, as they were European names and easy for him to pronounce. The surnames, however, were a different matter altogether, for they were our ancestral names and were therefore in our language. You would hear the minister saying 'Guniwe', 'Magadumeni' and 'Nomasele' instead of Goniwe, Magudumana and Nomazele. It was difficult to restrain ourselves from laughing, but we had to, as we were under strict instructions to be on our best behaviour as good Christian children.

The tickets were distributed quarterly to members of the church at the cost of three pennies for the children and a shilling for the adults. Everyone had to keep his or her ticket safe so that when one died, it would prove that one was a Christian and would therefore be welcome in Heaven.

⌇

A core value among African people is that *of ubuntu*. In defining *ubuntu*, empathy is a very important attribute. There is an idiom that says, '*Umntu ngumntu ngabanye abantu*', which means that the existence of a person depends on the existence of other people.

Another way of expressing that is: 'Completeness in the existence of a person is bound up with and satisfied by that person's interrelationship with other people.' *Ubuntu*, then, is expressed when people share what they have with those who do not have. The sharing is done in a manner that demonstrates respect for the recipients, ensuring that they always maintain their dignity.

Along those lines, there was a practice of lending out cattle, on condition that the beneficiary would look after them and see to their natural increase and then, after some years, the original cattle would be returned to the owner, leaving the increase (or, in current speak, profit) with the person who had been looking after the cattle. That culture of sharing prevented an uneven distribution of wealth and ensured a loyal commitment by all to the wellbeing of the community.

That practice of *ubuntu* is mentioned in the biography of O. R. Tambo, *Beyond the Engele Mountains*. In it, Tambo recalls a neighbour whose name was Nathinga (nothing). He was a new immigrant to the area who was allowed to stay at the Tambos with his family and helped to set up his home.

The home he was helped to set up was of the same quality as the other homesteads in the area. He was then given cattle to look after, according to the practice mentioned above. He was also given cornfields, which he cultivated to provide food for his family, just like any respectable man in the community.

Ubuntu underpinned every facet of our lives as we grew up. It was our biggest investment in each other as a community because we all needed to rely on our neighbours, and they needed to rely on us. For instance, if a young girl who was to be married had to be accompanied to her marital home, the returning delegation of those who had accompanied her would give a report back on how they had found the in-laws. If listening in, it is likely that one would hear the following, '*Hayi Noko, sifike ebantwini.*' Literally meaning, 'Yes, we found people there.' That does not refer to the form or the physical: the reference is to the essence: *ubuntu*.

These days, the term *ubuntu* has become overused, commercialised, trivialised and, in effect, denuded of its meaning. Consequently, I tend to steer clear of the concept. But when pressed to explain it, I find myself evoking the Xhosa poet, S. E. K. Mqhayi's concept of the three mischievous traits (*imichivase emithathu*), which are: *andazi*, *asindimi* and *andikhathali*. *Imichivase emithathu*, for me, represent what *ubuntu* is not:

Andazi	I do not know
Asindimi	It was not me
Andikhathali	I do not care

Those three are the direct antithesis of what *ubuntu* is. It is easier to illustrate what *ubuntu* is. My sadness is that I find that despite its espousal of *batho pele*, people first, a principle of *ubuntu*, our current government has become more and more characterised by the flouting of the very principles of *ubuntu*. With every approach to authority and power, ordinary people encounter *Andazi, Asindimi* or *Andikhathali*, or even all three.

Ilima is an expression of *ubuntu*, in its true form. Once in a while, a household in the *lali* would call *ilima*. I guess, in an urban context, one would refer to *ilima* as the equivalent of a thorough housecleaning, where neighbours are called to assist with the understanding that when it was their turn to call *ilima*, you too would be there to help out.

The house chores that were undertaken during *ilima* included weeding the mealie fields, collecting wood and cutting grass for thatching the roof. Those tasks were mainly done by women, although sometimes weeding was done by men, but that would always be specified in advance when extending invitations.

The community members knew that they had a responsibility to assist each other and to agree when invited. There was a saying among our people, *Izandla ziyahlambana*, which literally means 'hands wash each other'. There was reciprocity and a belief in the joy of shared work. Those who came to participate in *ilima* would bring their own working implements. In most instances, that would be a hoe used for weeding. While working, the women would sing in rhythm, mostly church choruses, and as they sang, the hoes would go up and down in unison.

It was important for the hostess to know beforehand how many people would be participating in *ilima* so that she could prepare sufficient refreshments for them. Basic food was prepared for *ilima*, so nobody would be prevented from calling one because they might not be able to provide refreshments for the participants. Usually, a drink called *marewu*, which is a fermented mealie porridge, was taken to the fields for the workers to drink and quench their thirst. After their hard work in the field, they would come back for the meal that would be served. Typically, the menu would be *umnqhusho* (stamped mealies and beans), *umbako* (homemade bread) and tea.

Ilima was one of the mechanisms for promoting household sustainability. Everybody in the community knew that if one expected to be assisted in one's time of need, one had to go out and assist the others, unless somehow incapacitated. In the townships, I found that women had created similar mechanisms, which they called *masingcwabisane* and *mroliswano*, or a combination thereof.

Masingcwabisane is a burial insurance fund run by women in a certain part of a township who come together to form a group and open a bank account into which each member deposits an agreed sum of money every month. The amount is not necessarily a big one but is a sum that can be afforded by all of the women. The working family members provide the money for the mother of the house to contribute to the fund. An agreed sum of money is withdrawn when a family member of the contributor to the fund dies, and the bereaved family uses the money for funeral preparations. As with *iilima* of the rural women, one had to be a regular contributing member to receive a withdrawn sum.

With *mroliswano*, the difference is that the membership consists of working women who pool funds together on a monthly basis. Each month, one member of the group will receive a lump sum of money. The cycle continues until everyone has received their part, and then it starts again. Usually, the membership is not more than twelve people, so that each month of the year, there is one woman who receives the lump sum. The amount of money contributed to that account is greater than that of *masingcwabisane*. Each member chooses a month when she will need a large sum of money, either for school fees and uniforms for her children or to buy a desired household item.

I believe that part of the reason the new democratic government has failed to make an impact on the lives of ordinary people in South Africa is because it has consistently distanced itself from them. Instead of building on the initiatives of the women on the ground, it consistently reduces women to beneficiaries of ill-considered programmes. Later, I will discuss that more fully, as I will list some of the programmes women had initiated at the grassroots level, which now no longer exist.

I do not remember much about my first day at school. I do, however, remember some of the incidents that occurred during my first year at school; and also, I knew generally how the first day of school started for the children of Ndunge. In Ndunge, there were no preschools or what are commonly referred to as crèches or Grade R. Children started school in Sub A.

I also remember that one's front milk teeth had to have fallen out before one could be admitted to school. As births took place at home, most of us in the village did not have birth certificates. Thus, to be admitted, the practice was that on the first day of school, every child who came to register had to grin to show the teacher their milk teeth, or lack thereof.

If the child's front milk teeth had not yet fallen out, the child would be told that they were still too young (*usemncinci*) and must go home and return the following year. That meant that on the first day of school, the disqualified children would have to wait outside, amusing themselves until classes were over, when they could walk back home with their siblings or neighbours. That did not happen to me because by the time I started school, I already had three siblings there, so they and MaNyathi knew how the system worked. I also remember that on my first day of school, I was well prepared with the required slate and pencil that had been purchased by MaNyathi.

Having siblings at school was very useful. During recess, the older children would check on their younger brother or sister. Sometimes, they would come with friends to show off their younger sibling. I remember an incident when my elder sister Nomvuzo came to me while I was playing with my peers during recess. She had something in her closed fist. She asked me to close my eyes and open my mouth wide. I did what I was told, and then Nomvuzo dropped something into my mouth. It was so little; it was soft and tasted of meat: it was a piece of ham. Nomvuzo had been given a piece of ham by her friend and classmate.

Nomvuzo's friend was a child who had been adopted by a lady who was a missionary in the village. As a result, she had all kinds of delicacies to share with Nomvuzo, which she in turn shared with me. The lady who had adopted Nomvuzo's friend was also the foster mother of many children from the worse-off families in the village, whom she brought up as her own. She was a missionary of the Full Gospel Church. I do not know what her real name was because she was simply referred to as Nkosazana, which means Miss or Ms but could also mean Princess.

∾

After I had passed Sub B, I was sent to Johannesburg to stay with relatives. Exactly how that came about, I did not know. Most likely, the relatives in Johannesburg had asked for me to come and stay with them. It was common during those days for families to share the responsibility of bringing up the children of their relatives. That arrangement had the added benefit of ensuring that the children had other children of their age group to play and grow up with. At the time, I was eight years old, and I had never travelled beyond our village. Neither had my siblings nor anyone my age that I knew. While most people left Ndunge to find work, I was leaving to live with my relatives and go to school in a different place – Johannesburg: *Egoli*, the place of gold!

I arrived at 234 Orlando East and discovered that my new family were the Mzaidumes. As mentioned, my Aunt Nontimbi Mda had married into that family. Aunt Nontimbi's daughter, Nokhathazwa, my cousin, was the same age as me, and the two of us were to be playmates. The family was staying with the *makhulu*, *uMakhulu* Phyllis Mzaidume, which meant that there was always an adult in the house to monitor and guide us.

Nokhathazwa and I attended school at the Law Palmer Memorial School, which was a Baptist school, even though we were Methodist. The Methodist School was situated in a very busy road, so *Makhulu* decided that it would be safer for us to attend the Baptist school.

Having gone to live in that Orlando East home exposed me to life in the city and the opportunities that children growing up there enjoy, such as educational tours, one of which was to the Pretoria Zoo. Pretoria would, much later, become my permanent home.

While living in Orlando East, I had the novel experience of going to the library to borrow a book. I would look over the books and choose the one that I wanted to read. Then, I would take it to the front desk where the librarian would write the details on my library card in her ledger. After that, she would stamp the paper affixed to the book with the date on which I was to bring it back. I was thus responsible for the book: I could read it, keep it safe and undamaged until the day I had to take it back to the library and choose another book if I wanted to. I learnt that I was responsible for returning the book, either before or on the day that was stamped on it. That was the most empowering feeling.

We also had the Girl Guide movement and our wonderful Brownies, which were like junior Girl Guides. Nokhathazwa and I would wear our little brown dresses and attend our Brownies meetings at the school. There were Sunday school sessions, too, which were similar to those I had participated in back in Ndunge. At the end of the year, I went home, and the expectation was that I would return for the next year. However, I had so missed home and wanted to be with my siblings that I asked Mama if I could stay there with her and my siblings instead.

I remember how happy I was to be back among the people who were so dear to me: Mama, Buti'Nyaniso, Sis'Noniwe, Buti'Mbulelo and Nomvuyelelo. But I missed Nomvuzo, the first of my siblings to pass away.

In some ways, I had changed, although I could not have found the words to describe how. I know that I had seen the ways in which people outside my world were materially better off in the city, and I had known instinctively that I still preferred being home among my people. Meanwhile, the conditions of my school in Ndunge had not changed. I had returned from Orlando East with a gym dress, a navy-blue blazer and a white shirt, which I could not use at school in Ndunge. None of the other children in the school had those luxuries, not even shoes. In solidarity, the parents who could afford to buy them did not, for they did not want to humiliate the children whose parents could not afford to do so. Therefore, all the children at school dressed simply in the type of clothing that could be afforded by all. What was most important was that everyone was neat and clean. Such was the *ubuntu* among the people of my community. But the conditions at school were quite difficult. For instance, there were no toilets, not even pit latrines. Instead, a secluded place was nominated for nature's call. Those places were differentiated into one area for the boys, another one for the girls and one for the teaching staff.

With the eyes of one who had returned from being away from them for the first time, I appreciated even more the extended family who surrounded me when I was in Ndunge. For instance, the family of my paternal uncle, his wife and their children: that family consisted of *Tat'omncinci* and *Ma'mncinci* (literally small father and small mother), and their names were *Tat'omncinc'uNomemez'exheni* and *Ma'mncinc'uMakhwetshube*. They had two sons and one daughter. I was always welcome in their home, which was just a stone's throw away from the school. When I did not walk in on my own initiative, I would be invited, with Mama's permission, to stay with them for a few days and be spoilt there. What was good was that I was encouraged to stay for as long as I liked and to go home when I felt like doing so. I was always welcome there and was considered to be a child of their home. I had missed them so much when I was in Johannesburg.

Theirs was a simple home, yet it was always filled with so much warmth, and they made me feel great. Truly, it was a loving and affirming environment. From the moment I entered that hut, there would be so much excitement. *Ma'mncinci* would welcome me, and she would say, 'Ntokazi (young lady), come and sit here, next to me.' She would be sitting on a grass mat by the fireplace and would place my elbow on her lap.

What I liked most was the stories I was told in that family. Each member participated in the storytelling. I found out that great storytellers are also good listeners. Always, when a story was being told, everyone would be quiet and listen, as if they were hearing the story for the first time. When I think of *Tat'omncinci* and *Ma'mncinci's* home, I always remember laughter, a hearty chorus of laughter.

The daughter of *Tat'omncinci* and *Ma'mncinci* was called Nomana, Sis'Nomana to me. She was a teacher by profession who taught at a *lali* outside Ndunge. She was a gifted storyteller, and I loved that the stories she told were about real people who looked like us and lived in villages like ours. She was so good at storytelling that I could almost see the people she was talking about: their clothes, their anger, their joy, their smiles. I will attempt to retell two of her stories for you. My skill at storytelling has never been as good as Sisi'Nomana's, but I will tell them as they were told to me and am sure that her stories are so good that they are spoilproof.

୬୬

In a village not very far away from here, there was a friendly white man who had served the community as a doctor for a long time. The villagers knew him well. Some had known him since his arrival in the village many years ago with his wife and their only daughter. Now that young girl had grown up and was to be married. The groom (*umkhwenyana*) and his family were not from the same village, so they would be travelling from far to attend the huge ceremony and fetch their *makoti* (bride). Everyone in the village was excited because the white doctor had invited people from the community to his daughter's wedding.

The majority of the guests were the teachers and other congregants of the

Full Gospel Church. The doctor and his family were Christian missionaries, as were the family of the groom. So every day for weeks before the ceremony, there was choir practice at the church. On some days, the doctor's wife and her team of seamstresses would take the measurements of the members of the choir for the purple tops and black skirts and pants they would wear to the wedding.

When the big day arrived, the choir's singing was so good that the Reverend declared that surely they were the choir of angels the scriptures spoke of. There were tears in the eyes of the doctor and his wife as they listened to the choir and looked at the beautiful bride who was their daughter.

After the wedding, when the rites had been completed, everyone was invited to the hall where dinner was to be served. Of course, many of the villagers did not pay much attention to that, as they expected to receive their refreshments outside the church, away from the bridal couple and their guests, who were mostly white people, which was the practice on such occasions. But as everyone was leaving the church, the doctor stood and explained that *everybody* was invited to join the bridal couple for the dinner reception. His daughter, the *makoti*, especially wanted to see the choir members so she could personally thank them for their performance during the church ceremony. That had been an incredible day with incredible events – and now this incredible thing! Everyone was invited to come and eat together!

That had never happened before, and so the whisperings began as each person wanted to confirm with the others that they had heard correctly. They asked each other, 'Did they say everybody, even us Blacks?' People were animated as they whispered back and forth on their walk to the hall where the dinner was to be served. *Imihlolo Ayi'pheli* (wonders never cease), they whispered as they shook their heads incredulously.

When the people walked into the hall, the host was standing at the door, 'Welcome! Welcome!' he shouted ecstatically, pointing to the elaborate buffet that had been laid out on the tables, which stretched out from one side of the hall to the other. 'You are welcome! Please, please help yourself to everything at the table. Please, please go ahead. Please …' he said, as he ushered them towards the buffet. That was yet another incredible thing. His guests, obeying him, grabbed the food in the serving dishes. Each took the serving dish in front of them, avoiding the green leaves. One guest would take the platter of meats, the other guest, the beautiful golden potatoes, another the rice or the beans, the beetroot and so on. Thus, the whole buffet of platters walked off the tables.

Embarrassed, some of the teachers and elders, who were more familiar with Western dining etiquette, attempted to stop the chaos and explain that there were empty plates available to enable each guest to dish out anything they liked into their own. The teachers then warned the guests that they would need to be careful to leave space for the best part of the *mcimbi* (occasion), which was the pudding with jelly and custard. For that, they explained, there would be small bowls to dish out into, and *ne cephe* (a spoon) with which to eat.

The gracious host thanked the teachers and elders for their assistance in bringing order to the proceedings. He told them, however, that they should not have worried, as he had been outside in the grounds and had seen little groups of the guests, sitting out in the grass, pooling together and sharing the food from the platter, just as he had observed them doing in their own homes. He too had, on occasion, partaken in that type of communal meal. However, he remarked that he suspected the advice about dishing out the jelly and custard in the bowls would be useful, as he doubted that one could share it in communal dishes the way the people of the village ate their meals.

The *umcimbi* continued well into the night because after the food and the speeches, there was more singing, although this time it was not church songs that were sung. And so, because of those songs – which were not of the church – there was also a lot of dancing!

Even today, when I think of Sisi'Nomana, I wonder at the stories she used to tell me, and I wish I could have asked her how she knew exactly which story I needed to hear at the time I needed to hear it. For instance, when I had returned from Johannesburg, I needed to hear the story about the white doctor's daughter's wedding. That story had made me proud of my people and the role they had played in the wedding ceremony and of the joy they had brought to the occasion. It had made me realise that different people did things differently and that our differences are to be celebrated as they are. They do not indicate that one is better than the other. Differences are fun.

The second story Sis'Nomana told me is a celebration of education. As I grew up, I found that there were different versions of this story, but they all revolve around the same theme: education.

This story takes place in our village, Ndunge, as divisions grew between those who had converted to Christianity, often referred to as the 'educated ones', and the 'ochre people' (*abambomvu*), those who had chosen to hold on to our people's traditions and our ways before we became 'civilised' (*singekaphucuki*). At the time, to my great sadness, those people were referred to as *amaqaba*, which is a derogatory term, mainly influenced by the Church. It would take a long time before people would understand that embracing Christianity did not mean one had to forsake one's tradition.

This is the story about Manelisi, who was born among the ochre people. Because they were termed *amaqaba*, they were often dismissed within the community as people who had no relevance. Manelisi was a very good student with a natural aptitude for every subject he was taught, be it maths, science, English, biology or geography. In fact, some of the teachers were worried that it was becoming too difficult to teach Manelisi. They were concerned that they no longer had the answers to some of his never-ending questions. Manelisi needed to go to a bigger school where the teachers would be able to cope with such a student. However, their appeals to the Church were not working. The reverend said that as Manelisi's parents were refusing to convert to Christianity, the Church could not assist with his education. That, even though Manelisi was the brightest student in the village, perhaps even in the whole of the Transkei.

Manelisi's parents and family were equally stubborn. The teacher suggested that they attend church and perhaps even agree to be baptised. The teacher said that they would only have to keep up the pretence long enough for Manelisi's college education to be paid for. Manelisi's family flatly rejected that suggestion. Were the teachers suggesting that they should be indebted to the people who derided them and their ways? The same people who called them heathens? Was the cost of their child's education to be him being taught to look down on his people unless they agreed to say they were what they were not? The parents said that they would work for the money to send their son to school themselves. Healdtown was the biggest town close to Ndunge and had a respected teacher training college. The parents said that they would send their son to that college once he had received his certificate from the secondary school in Ndunge.

So, once Manelisi had received his junior certificate at the secondary school, he went over to Healdtown for the teacher training course. All went well, and of course, Manelisi passed with excellent results and was now ready to return home and take up a teaching post at the secondary school in Ndunge. Ever thoughtful, he bought two trunks. He filled one with his clothes and the gifts he had bought for his parents to show his gratitude for their great sacrifices. The other trunk was filled with his books: his most treasured possessions. Manelisi boarded a bus from Healdtown, which would take him back to Ndunge; his trunks were put in a compartment at the back of the bus. The condition of the road between Healdtown and Ndunge was quite bad, and the bus he boarded was a sorry sight. It was, however, the only available transport between Healdtown and Ndunge.

On the way home, something happened to one of the wheels of the bus, causing it to veer off the road, narrowly missing a tree. The doors of the compartment with the luggage had been thrown open and some of the suitcases had fallen off. The passengers had to get out and they disembarked in shock because of what had almost happened, some praying and thanking God for their narrow escape. The people who lived in the houses along the road the bus had been travelling on came out and were also bearing witness and exclaiming how lucky the travellers were that no one had been hurt. They assisted with taking the luggage back to the bus and replacing the wheel so that it could continue its journey. When the damage had been repaired, the travellers were happy, and all seemed well.

When they got to Ndunge, however, only one of Manelisi's two trunks could be found in the compartment. He searched all over for the other one, even in the smallest crannies where he knew the trunk could not fit. Manelisi was distraught, but nothing could be done. The trunk with his books could not be found. His treasured possessions were lost, gone.

When he arrived home, Manelisi was in despair, even as he watched the joy shown by his parents upon receiving their presents. His mother noticed that and was worried. When he reported about the incident, she said, '*Kumnke kwa mfundro ka Manelisi waye yi hode eHealdtown* (All the education Manelisi has gathered at Healdtown has gone).' Manelisi's mother's words amused and strengthened him at the same time. He reassured his mother, telling her that only the books had gone and that those could be bought again, in time, while all he had learnt stayed with him and in him. That could only grow, and his plan was to grow it. He said that in time, he would travel the world, growing his education.

So, Manelisi started teaching in Ndunge and enrolling in education courses at Unisa. Upon finishing his basic degree in teaching, he travelled to the United Kingdom where he completed his Honour's degree, then his M.Phil. and then his Ph.D. During all that time, he was teaching in England, and then, they made him a professor. When Manelisi became a professor, the university invited his mother to attend his inaugural lecture.

At his request, the university asked Sis'Nomana to travel to England with his mother and serve as her translator during the trip. Manelisi's only request to Sis'Nomana was that she must make sure that she and his mother were clad in tradititional Xhosa attire for the event. And so, Manelisi's mother and Sis'Nomana travelled to England for the first time to attend Manelisi's inaugural lecture.

Manelisi's mother's first impression of England when they alighted at King's Cross Station was the greyness of London. She could not hide her disappointment. '*Kutheni inje lendawo? Uphila kanjani umta'am endaweni enje?* (Why is this place like this? How does my son live in a place like this?)'. But once they were out of the city in the countryside, she brightened up. England was a beautiful country. For now, it was also the place in which her son had made a home for himself. Wonders never cease. Here she was, *intombi yaMatolo*, having travelled by air to this place so far away, over the seas, where her son was now welcoming her!

They had a few days in which they could do as they liked, but all Manelisi's mother wanted to do, most of the time, was to sit down and listen to her son. For two days, they were mostly indoors, and the only language she heard was Xhosa. But then on the third day, they attended the lecture.

The hall where her son was to speak was huge, and it was full. Although most of the people were white, there were a few African faces in attendance. A few of them understood Xhosa, but most said they spoke other African languages. The tall and very dark man in a long dress said he spoke Wolof. Then a beautiful girl said that she came from Ethiopia and spoke Amharic. There were so many different African languages and African peoples. When the ceremony was about to begin, they were taken to their reserved seats, which were right in front of the podium.

The vice chancellor of the university opened the proceedings and welcomed the audience, taking time to specially welcome Manelisi's mother. Another man stood up and spoke of Manelisi, mentioning a long list of his publications and the valuable research he was working on. He then invited Manelisi to come forward and give his lecture. Everyone stood up and clapped as Manelisi walked up to the podium and took his place behind the microphone.

Manelisi greeted a lot of people as he started to speak, and then, he looked at his mother and spoke directly to her in Xhosa. After a pause, he mentioned to the audience his joy at having her present. Manelisi told them about his early days growing up in Ndunge and how the Church had refused to support his education unless he, but mainly his parents, abandoned their traditional practices and converted to Christianity. He spoke of how his parents had ensured that he could go and study at the teachers' college. He told of how the journey that led to him standing in front of them had started with him losing his trunk containing all of the books he owned. He described how he had been strengthened when reassuring his mother. She had been so desolate then, but he had assured her that all was not lost and that he was determined to travel the world and grow his education. He mentioned Sis'Nomana, who had travelled with his mother to attend this ceremony. He said that she was a brilliant teacher. He spoke with pride about how she was registered at Unisa to complete her first degree while also serving as the principal at a primary school in a village not far from his own. Manelisi told about working with Sis'Nomana and others to ensure that there were good learning institutions across the country.

When Manelisi stopped speaking, the applause was thunderous, and his mother was ecstatic. She kept saying to me '*Umvile, umvile? Ebethetha ngathi!* (Did you hear him? Did you hear him? He was talking about us!). Then she stood up, *wasina* (did a traditional dance), going up and down in front of the podium, all the time ululating and calling out Manelisi's clan names. The audience also stood up and clapped as they attempted to dance along. Then another man stood up and gave the vote of thanks and invited us to have refreshments just outside the hall.

When Sis'Nomana finished telling that story, she was silent for a long time, and she had a big smile on her face. I too was quiet for a while, and then I had a flood of questions that I rattled out all at the same time. 'Sis'Nomana,' I said, 'you are part of this story! How long did it take to go to England on the aeroplane? Were you scared?' and so on. When I stopped, she told me that I had asked many questions. She told me that maybe I should slow down, breathe and ask one question at a time, starting with the one I wanted answered most. So I was quiet for a while, and then it struck me: the thing I did not want and am most afraid of. I asked her, 'Sis'Nomana, are you going away? Are you going to go to England too? Are you going to leave me?' She looked at me for a long time, and then she replied, 'I said one question at a time, dear one, but I will answer them all, as they do go together.' Then she said to me, 'Yes, dear girl, I am going away. I am going to America, not England. I passed my junior degree; I was given a scholarship to study there. The flight that will take me to America stops in England for a short time before it goes to New York, where I will land. I will be away for a short time, only two years, but I will write to you about America, and I want you to write to me about you and Ndunge while I am away.

And that is how my first scrapbook began, full of postcards and letters from America.

⨏

The Sunday before she left, Sis'Nomana came to fetch me so we could go to an *umcimbi* that was being held at the village where she was principal of a lower primary school called Ntshamathe. Ntshamathe Lower Primary School had only one classroom. It took the ingenuity of the teaching team to ensure that, notwithstanding the one classroom, at all times during the school day, all classes would be in session. That meant that while one class occupied the only school room, the other three classes would take place outside, in the schoolyard, mostly under the shelter of the trees. As there were only two long benches available that could be carried outside, most of the children became adept at finding stones to sit on during the lessons.

When we arrived at the school, the whole village seemed to have come to wish my Sis'Nomana well for her journey over the seas. The teachers and learners had practised very hard to prepare a special concert for the occasion, and there were hilarious skits and much singing. At the end of the concert, one of the teachers stood up to thank Sis'Nomana on behalf of the parents and teachers of Ntshamathe Lower Primary School. He was a gifted speaker, perhaps that is why I still remember most of what he said, even now, and I recognise and appreciate his skill even more.

That teacher spoke about how the two years Sis'Nomana would be away would be a long time in the life of the school. For instance, there would be two sets of brand-new intakes, and the current Standard 1 and 2 learners would have left, hopefully to the Higher Primary School. Those were changes that were good and necessary in the life of the school. There were also changes that the speaker hoped for: changes that had been promised to the school and were yet to be fulfilled. Those were promises that Sis'Nomana had worked very hard to elicit fulfilment from the Transkei government.

'Now,' the speaker said, 'if *uTat'uMda apha* (if Mr Mda here), Principal of the Higher Secondary School, has made me a promise, I tell you, Principal Nomana, that when you return, you will find that what you were promised will be done for this school, done. But, my child,' he continued, addressing Sis'Nomana directly, 'I am old, and I am yet to see the eloquently made promises of the representatives of the Great Transkei government being kept.' He then directed his attention to the rest of the audience, saying that perhaps it was good that the school now had a young principal who was audacious and still had hope that the officials would keep the promises they had made to the people, especially when they would even come to the Great High Place (*Komkhulu*) to make those promises.

The speaker told us how when Sis'Nomana had heard that a high official from the government would be visiting *Komkhulu* in the village, she was determined to inform him about the school and the difficult conditions in which the children had to learn. Sis'Nomana had been aware that as a woman, and especially as a young woman, she had no hope of being admitted into the gathering, much less listened to. But Sis'Nomana was determined to be heard. So she had spoken with the women, who knew the ways of *Komkhulu*. Here, the different people in the audience had exchanged glances and laughed. Among them were the women who had conspired with Sis'Nomana.

The speaker told us how the women had come up with a plan to make sure that *uPrincipala wase Ntshamathe*, Sis'Nomana, was able to enter *Komkhulu* and be heard. That had required that the plotters bring *iinduna* into the plan. So it was that on the day of the gathering, clad in traditional Xhosa dress, *umbhaxo*, and looking regal, Sis'Nomana approached *Komkhulu*.

In keeping with the advice of the women, her co-conspirators, Sis'Nomana carried a bucket of water on her head as she walked towards the hut where the meeting with the representative of the government was taking place. The attendants gave her a wide berth, as they knew that this was the principal of the primary school, and they had been told that she would approach the gathering to have an audience with the chief.

On entering the door, Sis'Nomana removed the bucket from her head and held it with both hands at the level of her chest until she reached an opening where she could put it down. She had everyone's attention as she lowered the bucket onto the ground. At that point, a steward stood up and went to whisper in the chief's ear to brief him of the reason for Sis'Nomana's presence among them. The chief nodded as the steward spoke to him. Everyone else was quiet. Then the steward stepped back.

The chief looked at Sis'Nomana and said, '*Yiza, Ma'Mtolo, ndikwazise apha ku Mhlonishwa* ('Come, *Ma'Mtolo*, let me introduce you to this esteemed gentleman'). That was all Sis'Nomana needed, and so it was that she spoke to the representative of the Transkei government about the school, in front of *iNkosi*, *iinduna* and the elders. As she spoke, she thanked them for the opportunity to address the government representative who, in turn, thanked Sis'Nomana for the information she had shared with them and made a promise to *iNkosi* that he would send an official from the Department of Education who would come to the villlage to assess the needs of the school and make the appropriate arrangements for those to be attended to. '*Sisalindile*,' the speaker said. 'We are still waiting.'

Years later, when Sis'Nomana had returned from her sojourn over the seas, much later than she had promised, she told me that no one from the government had ever come to the village to attend to the school and its challenges as promised. Instead, the school committee had decided to extend the school themselves. When they were finished, they had three classrooms and a hut, which served as an office for the principal and the teachers.

⌇

I do not think that anyone ever outgrows the joy of hearing a good *ntsomi*. I have seen grannies like myself enjoying the telling of *iintsomi*. To this day, children enjoy listening to *iintsomi*. Even here, in the city, I have seen joy and wonder in the eyes of children as gifted storytellers like Gcina Mhlophe and her Zanebali collective tell them the stories we grew up with. I wonder what my grandmothers and their grandmothers would say if they were told that, all over the world, over the seas, women and men, girls and boys want to be told *iintsomi*.

I believe that every culture has a way of relaying its norms and values to its younger generation. In South Africa's rural areas, that was done through folktales, which also served as educational tools. In extended families, the role of storytelling fell to the grannies (fondly called *gogos* or *makhulus*), who were always hands-on in that significant part of childrearing. The folk stories they told were not necessarily accurate reflections of what had happened but represented ideas put together to mould the character and behaviour of the children. That moulding started as soon as the children could comprehend what was happening around them until the ages of ten or eleven.

In my experience, folk stories – *izinganekwane/iintsomi* (Zulu/Xhosa) are told around the fireplace after a hearty meal, just before bedtime. The meal would likely have been *umvubo* (a mixture of fermented milk [*amasi*] and ground, cooked corn [*inkobe*]). The grannies made sure that the characters in the stories were objects with which the children identified. Usually, the characters would be small creatures like ants and birds to depict diligence, cattle would show strength and might, while a fox would be used to indicate cunningness and opportunism.

Names that might sound ridiculous would be intentionally created to signify specific characteristics that the grandmother might want to discourage, such as laziness or greed. *Makhulu* might tell a story about a lazy girl called Notomboyi (remember, this was before women's rights activists drew attention to the biases in accepted gender roles). *Gogo* might say that Notomboyi was a very lazy child. She was so lazy that whenever she was sent to do anything, she would play sick. Mama would say, 'Notomboyi, could you please sweep for me?' And Notomboyi would say, '*Ndiyafa, Ndiyafa!* (I am dying, I am dying!).' If sent to fetch water, she would say, '*Ndiyafa, Ndiyafa!*' But always, at mealtimes, Notomboyi would be the first to jump up and dash towards the food, no longer complaining about any aches and pains. The antics of Notomboyi were to illicit a strong disdain for laziness and encourage diligence.

Every story had a similar introduction that would capture the attention of the listeners: *kwasukela ngantsomi,* meaning 'from a myth'. That would hook the children's undivided attention, and complete silence would signal their readiness to hear the story. That introduction would be followed by the phrase: Long, long ago, in a far away country …

A good storyteller would use voice inflections for dramatic effect: at appropriate moments in the narrative, the voice would rise to a well-conceived crescendo, followed by a riveting diminuendo. The storyteller might break into song to reflect an avian character, while the roar of a fierce wild animal would be unmistakable in the deep fluctuating resonance of a guttural tone. A timely whisper might signal the gripping climax.

Without doubt, the art of storytelling, as developed by the *gogos*, compares favourably with some of the finest theatrics of the thespian world. The storyteller's use of voice control can evoke the whole gamut of emotions in children: from joy to fear and from exuberance to melancholy. The storyteller would then mollify the aroused feelings of the children by toning down her voice and reassuring them that, fortunately, the particular animal mentioned loved children. Thus, calm would be restored. Generally, *intsomi* would go on until Granny announced the end with the phrase, *Phela, phela, ngantsomi* (And so the story ends).

Iinstomi can never be told during the day, as there is a superstition that if that happened, horns would grow on the foreheads of both the narrator and the listeners. However, my grandmother taught us a unique chant that we could use to confuse the horns so that, on exceptional occasions, *Makhulu* could tell us *iintsomi* during the day. If *Makhulu* believed that we had been very good and had done something to make her proud of us, she would reward us by saying that on that one occasion, she would tell us *iintsomi*. Then we would gather around her and, in unison, we would chant: '*Mpondo phuma'pha, ungapumi apha, mpondophum'apha ungaphum' apha*' ('Horn grow here, do not grow here; horn grow here, do not grow here'). Over and over we would chant, while pointing our fingers on one side of our forehead, telling the horn to grow there and then pointing to the same side of the forehead and telling the horn not to grow there. On and on we would repeat the chant, alternating from one side of the forehead to the other, until the horns were thoroughly confused, not knowing where to grow. Then, when *Makhulu* knew that the horns were truly confused and would not be able to grow on our foreheads, she would begin: '*Kwasukela ngantsomi.*'

Some stories were humorous, evoking giggles and laughter. In addition to providing entertainment, *iintsomi* enabled Granny to monitor whether the children were responding as expected.

Very young children always felt good and were excited and entertained by *Makhulu's iintsomi*. As they grew older, they would start offering opinions about some of the characters depicted in the stories. They would also begin to ask questions. *Makhulu* would listen, looking out for signs of the development of reasoning ability and logic. There would be questions like, 'Granny, why is it that the animals do not speak now?' Granny would reply, 'But I told you at the beginning: it was long, long ago. Animals could talk then, and it was in a country very far away, not here.' Those questions were important to Granny because they provided a way of assessing a child's cognitive development.

Stories could also be used as a valuable mechanism to create awareness about potential dangers and steer children away from possible harm. For instance, there was a big fig tree by the stream at the bottom of our mealie field. Most of the time, the stream was dry, and one would see only a layer of rock beneath the fig tree. The figs of that tree were delicious; they even grew on its trunk. The children were warned not to go near the tree because it was dangerous. To ensure that that message stuck, we were told a story that discouraged us from going near it. It went like this: Once, a very long time ago, there was a herdboy who was very strong. That herdboy had ignored the warnings about the fig tree and had climbed it to pluck its figs. While he was up there, a branch broke from the tree, and the boy came tumbling down. His head struck the rock, and his brains were scattered all over.

That story was known by all the children of the community. It was passed down from generation to generation and, as far as I know, no one has dared to go near that tree. It is unknown whether that unfortunate incident had actually happened, but the story worked as an effective deterrent.

Children were also exposed to positive developmental influences that taught them some important life lessons, as many of the stories would have a moral and reflect the social precepts of the family and community. In that way, by the time a child went to school, they would have been socialised to consider every adult as their parent, who must be respected. That was one of the critical roles fulfilled by *Makhulu*. She may not have been in a position to assist her grandchild with homework but would have prepared the child adequately for the teacher to work with. These are some of my *Makhulu's iintsomi*. My gift to you.

⁂

Kwasukela ngantsomi. Long, long ago, in a faraway country, there lived a mother frog who lived with her five little ones in a stream. Mama frog taught them how to survive both inside and outside of the water. The little ones loved to play games. One of their favourite games was jumping in and out of the water while making a big SPLASH sound. Splash, the water went as they jumped. Splash! Splash! The little frogs enjoyed hearing that sound and would compete to see who could make it the loudest. They were a very happy family.

One day, Mother-frog decided to leave the children for a while and explore downstream. While she was away, a herd of cattle came to the stream to drink. It was a very hot day, and the cattle were very thirsty. In their mad rush to get to the water, they stomped on the little frogs with their big feet. Tragically, all but one of Mama's little froggies died. That lucky little frog had managed to jump into the water just in time to avoid the stampede.

When Mother frog came back, she was shocked when she saw the mashed little bodies of her children. She got very angry and wanted to know who had killed her little ones. Just then, the surviving little frog appeared. Breathless and scared, the little one said, 'A big dragon – my sisters, quak-quak.' Mother frog continued her questioning, 'Quak——k how big was it, as big as this?' While asking that question, she inflated her abdomen to extend the size of her body. The little frog said, 'No, Mama, I did not see where its body started and where it ended. It was so very huge, quak.' Mother frog did not listen and inflated her body again and again, all the time asking, 'Quack, this big?' Suddenly, there was a big explosion as Mother frog burst. And that was her end. The little frog cried and jumped back into the stream, left all alone. '*Phela, phela, ngantsomi* (That is the end of the story).'

A more contemporary story is about the wonderful inventions of the world.

Kwasukela ngantsomi. In a land far, far away, children who worked very hard were sent to a special college. There, they were organised into groups based on their area of interest. One group loved learning of faraway lands and listening to tales about the amazing inventions that could be found there. One day, to assess how much the children in her class had learnt, the wise woman teacher asked them to tell her what they thought were the most wonderful inventions in the world. Though there were some disagreements, the following list emerged:

The Great Pyramids of Egypt
The Taj Mahal
The Grand Canyon
The Panama Canal
The Empire State Building
St Peter's Basilica
The Great Wall of China

While compiling that list, the teacher noticed that one student was not participating in the exercise. So she asked the girl if she did not want to contribute to the discussion. The girl replied 'Yes, but I can't quite make up my mind. There are so many.' The teacher said, 'Well, tell us what you have and maybe we might help.'

The girl hesitated and then began voicing her thoughts. 'I think the things I treasure most in the world are the following senses: to see, to hear, to touch, to taste, to feel, to laugh and to love.' The room fell silent. It was so quiet you could have heard a pin drop. *Phela, phela ngantsomi.*

Then, there was another story about tiny frogs, which goes like this. *Kwasukela ngantsomi.* Once, there was a bunch of tiny frogs who had arranged a competition. The objective was to reach the top of a high wall: whichever tiny frog got there first would be declared the winner. A big crowd had gathered around the wall to see the race and cheer on the contestants.

The race began. Honestly, no one in the crowd believed that the tiny frogs would reach the top of the wall. One could hear such statements as, 'Oh, way too difficult! They will never make it to the top!' or, 'Not a chance, they will not succeed. The wall is too high.'

The tiny frogs began collapsing and, one by one, they started falling off the wall. The crowd continued yelling, 'It is too difficult! No one will make it!' More tiny frogs got tired and gave up. But one little frog continued climbing higher and higher and higher. That one would not give up.

At the end, every one of them gave up, except that one little frog who continued climbing the wall … all the way up until it reached the top. All of the other frogs were surprised and wanted to know how that one frog managed to do it. Finally, after a while, when all of the questions remained unanswered, it became evident that the frog that had succeeded was deaf, and therefore it had not heard the negative remarks of the onlookers. Thus, the little frog could remain focused and continue climbing until it reached its goal, undeterred by all the naysayers.

The next story is a variation of one of Aesop's Fables. *Kwasukela ngantsomi.* In a village far away, a couple went to the market and bought a donkey. On their way home, they came across a boy who was walking along the same road. The boy commented, 'How very stupid. Why does neither of them ride on the donkey?' Upon hearing that, the couple stopped, and the husband decided that the chivalrous thing would be to let his wife ride the donkey. So, he helped his wife onto the donkey and walked next to them. On they went.

A short distance ahead, an old man saw the man walking next to his wife who was riding the donkey. His comment was, 'Surely, that is not right. The husband is the head of the family, so how can that woman, his wife, ride on the donkey while her husband is on his feet?' On hearing that, the wife quickly got down and insisted that the husband ride the donkey, and she would walk beside them. And thus, they continued.

Further along the way, they met an old lady. She was amazed at the scene: the man riding the donkey and the lady walking next to them. She commented: 'Clearly, that is no gentleman. How can he ride on the donkey and make his wife walk? He is not a gentleman.' On hearing that, the husband asked his wife to join him on the donkey. And on they went, this time with both of them riding the donkey.

Then they met a young man walking along the road. 'Poor donkey,' the young man said. 'How can you hold up the weight of two people? They are cruel to you.' The husband and wife immediately climbed down from the donkey and decided that they would carry it on their shoulders. That, it seemed to them, was the only choice left. So, on they went, the man and the woman, carrying the donkey on their shoulders.

Later on, while the couple were balancing gingerly on a narrow bridge with the donkey hoisted on their shoulders, the donkey looked down from that high vantage point – past the woman's and man's shoulders, past the narrow bridge, all the way down to the river. The donkey got frightened and began to struggle. In that struggle, all three lost their balance and fell into the river. *Phela, phela, ngantsomi!*

☙

After completing Standard 6, I had to leave the Eastern Cape, as there were few institutions for higher education there. I was very grateful when I was accepted to do my secondary studies at Saint Lewis Betrand's in Newcastle, KwaZulu-Natal Province, which was a Catholic institution. At that time, I had to go with a cousin, Buti'Lindwa Mzaidume, who was a teacher there. He was the son of *Dadobawo* u'Nontombi Mda. As mentioned, I had stayed with *Dadobawo* and her family in Orlando East, as a little girl.

Initially, all was good at Saint Lewis. I appreciated the strict and caring attitude of the nuns who ran that institution. Every morning before classes, we had fitness exercises out in the open. Those were invigorating and gave us sufficient energy and *vuma* (allowed) for the demanding school day ahead.

Yes, all was well until the last week of May. Oh, it was so, so cold! For the first time, I experienced frost-covered mornings. In class, I had a difficult time holding a pen to write, as my fingers were stiff and cold. My fingers were stiff and my nostrils would water, nonstop. When the June holidays came, what a relief. I could go home for a break, away from that freezing cold, which was becoming debilitating.

During the first days at home, I felt much better, and at first, I could assist with the household chores. It was harvest time, and there was so much to be done in the fields. But just a week before the end of the holidays, I fell seriously ill. My joints became swollen, and moving was difficult. My mother thought the illness was due to the cold winter I had experienced in Newcastle and took me to the doctor in Bizana who diagnosed it as rheumatic fever. I was warned not to do strenuous work, as that would make my heart stop, which would be the end of me.

The doctor advised that I should not go back to school for the remaining half of that year. After a few follow-up visits, he introduced a regimen of weekly injections, for which I had to go into town.

Mr Zietsman, who was a local general dealer, stopped at my home, once a week, on his way to the village to give me a lift to the doctor's place. That favour was offered to my family because we were good customers of his, as his shop was in our *lali*. Mr Zietsman drove an open van. If it had been an ordinary car, it would not have been possible for him to take me to the doctor because of the laws of the time. A Black girl seated in a car with a white man, regardless of the age difference, would have amounted to a contravention of the Immorality Act.

Mama's instructions were very clear as to what I was to do. She told me, '*Nomasomali mtanami*, this *mlungu* (Nomasomali my child, this white person), Mr Zietsman, has agreed to take you to the doctor for your injections. He will stop in front of our home at ten in the morning, so you must be outside the house at that time. When Mr Zietsman arrives, you must jump onto the van at the back.' Mama was adamant that 'There is no need for you to greet him or speak to him, my child. At the village, he will stop at the Post Office. When that happens, you will get off the van and walk to the doctor's surgery (consultation rooms). When you have had your injection, walk back to the post office. If the van is not there, wait for it to return from the bakery.' And so it was, every week for the rest of the year.

Every time Mr Zietsman arrived, I would jump onto the van at the back, and I would sit there until we reached Bizana and stopped at the post office. Then, I would go to the doctor's office, receive my injection and walk back to the post office where I would find Mr Zietsman's van parked outside. Mr Zietsman would be sitting in his van waiting for me, having already collected the provisions for his shop. Once he heard the thud at the back of the open van as I climbed in, he would know that his passenger had arrived and would drive me back home. Once there, I would jump off and Mr Zietsman would proceed on his way.

There was never any communication between Mr Zietsman and me, not a word. Such was the manner of apartheid. That was considered normal and it was wise to accept that that was the way things were. We made use of those 'favours' because they were expedient.

During my time at home, I started to learn about something that had been rendered invisible to us as children growing up: the whisperings about what had been a long and arduous war of dispossession that had lasted for over a century. That long war had left our people forced onto a small space of land and compelled to send men to seek work in the mines and on the farms of those who now 'owned' the dispossessed land of our people.

Although the war had been lost and all non-agricultural ways of living, including cotton processing and iron smelting, had been virtually decimated, battles continued to take place in the cramped conditions in which people were forced to live. At times, the battles would turn inwards, among people who had known each other for a long time. That was because the new 'chiefs' who had been created by the colonialists would engage in battle with our people and *iinkosi*. The 'chiefs' created by the colonialists were part of an elaborate method of administering the colonies. Consequently, there would be protracted battles. *Iinkosi* and their men would be engaged in a proxy war with the chiefs and tribes created by the colonialists. By confronting those pseudo chiefs, they were in fact fighting the unjust laws of the government that had deprived them of their rights. Those battles tended to be fought in isolated places, far from the communities; hence, the name, *Nonqulana*, in reference to the places where the battles were fought. The tribesmen would use clubs, sticks and spears. The *abelungu* would also enter the fray, dropping stuff from helicopters, which, it was said, caused the tribesmen to drop down and die. At best, it would make their eyes water and burn and their whole body burn and itch very badly.

In the patriarchal society in which we lived, those things were considered matters that concerned men and were never talked about to children. Invariably, however, things would come to a boil and children and women, who were not privy to much of the debate and discussions, including details of the ongoing conflict, would be pulled into the fray. For example, on occasion, the sense of anger against the government and those who were viewed as colluding with it rose so high that there would be attacks on the households of those in the community who were considered to be in the employ of the government.

Because in my family there were two teachers, public servants, and our neighbours also had teachers in their families, it was decided that it would be safer for us if we all slept in the mielie field at night, instead of in our houses. And so it was that I remember being carried in the dark to the mielie fields, to be protected in case our home was torched. But much of the details of the occurrences of the time are vague in my memory.

So much later, I wanted to make sense of what had been happening in emaMpondweni when I was growing up – which, at the time, had been the the subject of whisperings around me. I wanted to know what that stuff was that the white men had thrown out of the helicopters. It had all sounded unbelievable to me.

When I was older and reading and researching, I found among the writings of Govan Mbeki and others corroborations of the *Ngquza-Nonqulana,* as Mama had said – and the reference to the massacre at Nongquza. I include here one of the reports on the Mpondo Revolts that I came across.

The Mpondo Revolts: 1950–1960s
(Extract from the South African History Archive)

The Ngquza Hill Massacre represents the height of revolts against the white apartheid state known as the Mpondo Revolts. The Mpondo Revolts were a series of rebellions and resistances to the apartheid government's policies in the 1950–1960s. One of the reasons given for these revolts is the Rehabilitation/Betterment Scheme. The Betterment Scheme was a result of the Native Trust and Land Act, which came into being in 1936. This Act led to the establishment of the South African Native Trust (SANT), which sought to purchase additional land which would increase the 7% prescribed by the Natives Land Act of 1913 to 13% of the South African land surface. In 1939, the state embarked on a policy of conservation measures known as 'Betterment'. This scheme was about resettlements, stock control, rotational grazing, fencing of grazing land, culling, regular dipping and promotion of government-sponsored cattle sales. The scheme was implemented by magistrates in the villages, but they were met with 'cold silence' in the early 1940s. However, it was in 1947 that it was first applied to the Transkei in Butterworth. The first resistance to the rehabilitation happened in Mount Ayliff as early as 1942. The amaXesibe formed an organisation known as iKongo, which sought to fight to protect their land in 1947. IKongo would later be adopted in Pondoland as the Mpondo people wanted to protect their land from the South African government in the 1950s and 1960s.

The Bantu Authorities Act of 1951 deepened the resistance to the Betterment Scheme. The introduction of the Act meant that the tribal leaders were the extended arm of the South African apartheid government. The chiefs were used to implement the plans of the state and were less accountable to the people. Additionally, the system increased taxes, shifted away from elected authority and saw a reduction in popular participation. The Bantu Authorities system was imposed from outside with little consultation with the people of Pondoland. Chiefs were also known to accept bribes from the government and private companies in return for allotting people land. In early March 1960, thousands of Mpondo people gathered in various parts of Pondoland on the day the apartheid government-created Isisekelo Tribal Authority was due to begin operations in Bizana. The movement became known as Intaba (Mountain), when it was not called iKongo, because it hosted its meetings on mountainous areas.

Some members of iKongo, such as Anderson Ganyile, were ANC members, but there was no evidence that the movement had any affiliations to the ANC. While the initial meeting was held in Bizana at Mount Nonqulwana, other mountains/hills like Ngquza, Nqindili and Ndlovu also hosted meetings. Wealthy individuals such as chiefs and traders were expected to contribute large sums to the movement, while evangelists and teachers who had been politicised through Bantu Education took leadership roles. It became apparent to the iKhongo/mountain committees that there were government agents within their ranks and their activities were reported to the magistrates. The iKongo agreed that if these members did not co-operate, they would be burned or killed. Between March and June 1960, late ANC stalwart Govan Mbeki reported that 27 kraals and 22 people, including two chiefs, headmen, five police informants and bodyguards were burnt.

On 6 June 1960, thousands of Mpondo tribesmen heeded a call for a mass meeting to discuss the violence in Pondoland, as well as the Bantu Authorities Act of 1951 and the Betterment Scheme at Ngquza Hill between Flagstaff and Lusikisiki with the iKongo. The meeting was disrupted by airplanes which dropped smoke bombs and teargas while armed police officers surrounded the meeting. Although the people at the meeting raised a white flag to signal peace, the police opened fire. Eleven people were killed, 58 were injured and 23 arrested.

Shortly after the massacre, violence broke out in the Flagstaff District where a police patrol was ambushed and stoned by angry Mpondo people. The police retaliated by shooting at them. Two police officers were injured and one headman was arrested. In November 1960, further violence by police disrupted a meeting in Ngqindile near Flagstaff. The Chief and his indunas (headmen) were violently killed, others were wounded and ten huts in the kraal were burnt down. Several violent clashes took place in Bala near Flagstaff, and police officials were rushed to the area while military aircraft monitored the meeting by hovering over the mountains. After the massacre, a commission of inquiry was set up in mid-July to investigate the Ngquza Hill Massacre and hear the grievances of the people of Eastern Pondoland. The Mpondo people demanded the removal of Bantu Authorities, the removal of Paramount Chief Botha Sigcau, a relief from taxes and representation in the South African government. On 11 October, the commission of inquiry declared to a group of 15,000 people that the grievances of the people of Pondoland were unacceptable. On 25 October, a meeting of 6,000 people rejected the findings of the commission and initiated a boycott of white traders. On 1 November 1960, all white businesses were boycotted in Bizana. The boycott ended in January 1961.

The Bantu Authorities System collapsed in Bizana, Lusikisiki and Flagstaff in mid-July 1960. The Mountain Committee, iKongo, took over the local judicial and administrative functions in the absence of chiefs. They set up people's courts, allocated land and hut sites and punished the informers and supporters of the Tribal Authorities System. In September 1960, the iKongo organised a census boycott and sent a petition to the United Nations.

On 30 November 1960, the South African apartheid government declared a State of Emergency in Flagstaff, Bizana, Ntabankulu, Lusikisiki and Mount Ayliff. Entrance to these districts without a permit was prohibited. The government blocked all entrances to these towns. Chiefs and headman were granted more power and any rebellion was suppressed. Thirty people were sentenced to death and only nine of these sentences were cancelled.

In March 1997, Ngquza Hill Massacre survivor, Clement Xabu, addressed the Truth and Reconciliation Commission. Xabu described the gathering as peaceful and narrated the terror around the massacre. 'Some of us were able to run into the forest. There were people around the whole mountain shooting at us. People were injured. We carried 58 people to … a house. Eleven were killed instantly,' Xabu said. A monument which cost R15 million was erected in honour of the victims of the Ngquza Hill Massacre.

ᘔ

Looking back, I realise that Mama took advantage of the period when I was laid off school to teach me and plant in me a curiosity about the history of our people. For instance, Mama was a staunch Christian woman, and it was from her that I would hear for the first time about Tiyo Soga. I took a keen interest in reading about the life of Tiyo Soga, the fascinating discourse of his writings and the debates about him generated in the Methodist Church, particularly among theologians like Reverend Mpumlwana, a contemporary of Steve Biko, and Professor Barney Pityana. Those discussions that they pursued about the Church, Blackness and identity interest me greatly.

The hymn *Lizalis' idinga lakho,* written by Reverend Tiyo Soga

Lizalis' idinga lakho (Fullfil/realise your promise),
Thixo Nkosi yenyaniso (Faithful/Truthful God)!
Zonk' iintlanga, zonk' izizwe (All races, all nations)
Ma zizuze usindiso (Must be saved).

Amadolo kweli lizwe (All knees in this world)
Ma kagobe phambi kwakho (Must bow before you),
Zide zithi zonk' iilwimi (So that all tongues)
Ziluxel' udumo lwakho (Proclaim your glory).

Law'la, law'la, Nkosi, Yesu (Govern/Prevail our God)!
Koza ngawe ukonwaba (Happiness can only come through you);
Ngeziphithi-phithi zethu (Because of our struggles/challenges),
Yonakele imihlaba (The world is damaged).

Bona izwe lakowethu (Look at our world),
uxolel' izoono zalo (Forgive our sins);
Ungathob' ingqumbo yakho (Do not send your wrath)
Luze luf' usapho lwalo (To kill the children).

Yaala, Nkosi, singadeli (Prohibit us God from disobeying)
Iimfundiso zezwi lakho (The teachings of your Word);
Uze usivuselele (Revive us).
Sive inyaniso yakho (We can hear your Truth).

I also got to hear about my father, Lenford Goniwe, and the kind of person he had been. I learnt from Mama about his seminal hymn, *Lizali'idinga lakho*, which I truly love. Mama also told me that he had been a shop assistant at Milton's general store in our village, Ndunge. Mr Milton, my father's employer, was called *Nkom'nophondo* by the villagers, which means 'the cow has a horn'.

In those days, being a shop assistant meant that my father was in a strategic position. He met with people from various social strata and regions of Bizana and its hinterlands. They, in turn, would use him as a nodal point where they would leave messages and packages to be picked up by their peers, as they too passed through Ndunge. In this manner, my father, Tat'uLenford Goniwe met Tat'uOliver Reginald Tambo. Tat'uO. R. used to come to the shop four times a year when he was on his way from Johannesburg going home to Kantolo, his *lali*, or when he was returning from Kantolo on his way to Johannesburg. *Nkom'nophondo's* was also conveniently placed with a view of the goods shed called *gushede* by the local people. On many occasions, Tat'uO. R. would go to Tat'uLenford while waiting for a message from someone arriving at *gushede* or to meet with many a young person who would travel with him to Johannesburg to start his or her training there.

When all of that started, according to Mama, my eldest brother Buti'Nyaniso was still in primary school. When Buti'Nyaniso was ready to go to secondary school, Tat'uTambo had already recommended him to go to St Peter's in Rosettenville where he was teaching. And so it happened that my brother Buti' Nyaniso became a student at St Peter's and travelled with Tat'uTambo, every year, to and from Johannesburg.

Mama said that my father had been very impressed by that educated gentleman whom he also praised as being a Christian with integrity.

✒

At the beginning of the following year, I continued my formal education at the Ohlange Institution in Durban. That institution was founded by one of the first presidents of the ANC, John Langalibalele Dube. The school was built with funds from the American Board Mission, so it was a missionary institution. The school's history created a strong feeling of pride and belonging in the students. There is a school anthem, *Mafukuzela onje nge Zulu,* which is sung by the generations of students who acquire education there. Nelson Rolihlahla Mandela, who was to become the first president of Democratic South Africa, cast his very first vote at Ohlange in 1994.

When I arrived at Ohlange, the founder, Langalibalele Dube had long before passed on. At the time, the school was struggling financially as the donor funds had dried up. Despite that, it steadfastly continued to accept children from poor communities, and no student was sent home for failing to pay their school fees.

My school fees were paid by my eldest sister, Sis'Guda, who was a primary school teacher at kwaNdunge. At the beginning of the school year, every student was expected to pay a portion of the fees, which would enable the students to receive the books required for their studies for that year. I was one of those students who had to wait until month-end before that portion of my fees could be sent from home. By the time the money arrived, my classmates had covered a lot in their studies, and I had to work very hard to catch up.

My most endearing memory of that institution is of the Sunday evening service, which would be conducted by the members of the academic staff who looked splendid dressed in their academic regalia. The school had two choirs that were composed of students: the senior choir and the junior choir. Those choirs were also conducted by staff members.

Ohlange was a Christian School that brought together young women from different provinces and instilled in them a deep sense of commitment to public service. I met many of the friends I am still in contact with at Ohlange. Many of the girls proceeded to King Edward with me. Over the years, we were to meet others, go our separate ways and sometimes meet again as we travelled our different journeys. Interestingly, as I look back, I see that what we had in common, notwithstanding our different career choices, was our common dedication to public service.

When I finished at Ohlange, I had already decided that I wanted to become a nurse. When I discussed that with Mama, I discovered for the first time that my father had vowed that none of his children would become nurses. Mama said that my father's experience with nurses in his life had led him to a very low opinion of the profession. I was not shocked at that negative impression of people in the nursing profession, as it was very common among my people. But at Ohlange, I had glimpsed among my peers a commitment to transform the institution based on an understanding we shared that nursing was an important profession that had the potential of enabling one to assist those in need, in very meaningful ways.

Despite my late father's pledge to the contrary, Mama said that she was going to allow me to study nursing. Her reasons for doing so were purely practical. She said that nursing as a profession had the advantage that I could earn a living while studying. Mama also said that there was no money to pay for me to go into teaching and, at that stage, three of my siblings were already teachers. She suggested that I could send her some of the stipend – the money I would earn while in training – to assist her with some of the household essentials. I was so relieved and grateful. I assured Mama that I would send the money and that I would always be kind and respectful to the patients.

As she always did when crucial decisions were taken, Mama prayed for me. She prayed that God would protect me on my journey and in my studies. In hindsight, it seems to be that Mama's prayer for me is reminiscent of the Nurses' Creed, which I would take at the end of my training.

Nurses' Pledge of Service

I solemnly pledge myself to the service of humanity and will endeavour to practise my profession with conscience and with dignity.
I will maintain, by all the means in my power, the honour and noble tradition of my profession.
The total health of my patients will be my first consideration.
I will hold in confidence all personal matters coming to my knowledge.
I will not permit consideration of religion, nationality, race or social standing to intervene between my duty and my patient.
I will maintain the utmost respect for human life.
I make these promises solemnly, freely and upon my honour.

All of my elder siblings had pursued teaching as a profession, which had enabled them to assist with the household needs while also educating us younger siblings. Nursing was viewed with suspicion at home and in our *lali* because of the people's experiences with hospitals and nursing at the time. So, I think that is why I always carried an internal scale upon which I constantly compared the two professions, seeking to put nursing above teaching as a profession. Clearly, there is no value in such a comparison – especially as I know that this country needs good teachers and good nurses.

But back then, having benefited from the input of my teacher siblings for all of my needs, including my education, I must have had a big chip on my shoulder. So I compared the two and was naturally biased towards nursing. It seemed to me, then, that between the two professions, the conditions for nurses were better than the conditions for those in the teaching profession.

First, the curriculum for Black nursing trainees was the same as that of their white counterparts, although the institutions the Black nurses and the white nurses attended were segregated. With teaching, to my knowledge at least, the curriculum of the Black teacher trainees was different from that of their white counterparts.

Second, as the sister of three siblings who had entered the teaching profession, two of whom were young women, I knew, first-hand, how rough conditions could be for young women in the profession. One of the reasons was that after completing their training, those young women had no choice as to where they would teach. Often, they were sent to teach in villages very far from their homes. Once there, alone in an unfamiliar place, a young woman would have to stay with people who were strangers to her so she could be near to the school she had been sent to. Some of them would be abused by their hosts in various ways, which they would have to endure in silence.

A teacher who raised problems or pointed to the difficulties they were encountering due to their living circumstances was likely to be expelled, and that would reflect as a failure on their part. Another challenge experienced by young women in the teaching profession is that once they got married, they had to resign from their teaching post. That is one of the reasons people living in the rural areas preferred to educate their sons rather than their daughters. Nursing had the advantage that one was always with a team of peers who became very close, living in the same quarters. Upon finishing one's training, there were always nurses' quarters at the hospital and nurses you had trained with, wherever you went.

Once I started nursing, however, I was quickly disabused of the rose-coloured lenses through which I had looked at the profession from the outside. Nursing was not immune to our apartheid reality. When we started in 1961, our group, A61, had 68 young aspirant nurses in that intake. In 1964, when we completed, there were only nine of us: Nomtuse Mbere, Rose Lawrence, Ntsiki Diko, Patricia Misha, Winifred Zama, Irene Rini, Helen Banda, Dudu Msomi and me. It was true that all of us, *blankes* and *nie blankes*, wrote the same exams, but not one of the 59 who were expelled were expelled for attaining bad grades. Our exams were all marked together, and one could not infer the race of the writer from the exam script. Consequently, it was during the practicals, when officials from the Nursing Council Headquarters in Pretoria came to conduct the practical exams, that the wholesale culling took place. I have no idea how the nine of us survived.

Apartheid was deeply entrenched when it came to the renumeration of public servants and, nurses, like teachers, were not immune. The much-touted stipend I was so looking forward to turned out to be seven pounds, six and seven (£7,67) for African trainee nurses. As a qualified nurse, I could look forward to earning ten pounds (£10)!

I trained as a nurse at King Edward VIII hospital in Durban. Three months before we began attending lectures, the group I was in began our trial nursing period. During that time, we were placed in the hospital wards to learn the routine we would have to follow as nurses in the hospital. As mentioned, I belonged to the group of intakes referred to as A61. I was placed in Hut 2, which was a children's medical ward. Some of the children we received at that ward came from the shanty towns on the outskirts of Durban. The ward was always full of children in cots and some in bassinets. The first three days of that trial nursing period comprised the most challenging time of my entire nursing career. Luckily, there were senior nurses who were always there to guide the 'new ones', as we were called.

Each morning, when we came in at seven-thirty, we had to bathe the children and change the linen. My first task was to take the babies from the bassinets and place them on a table at the centre of the ward that had been prepared for the baby baths. To my horror, for the first three consecutive days, at least one of the babies I would bring to the table for bathing would turn out to be lifeless. On such occasions, I would have to call a senior nurse to look at the baby and, invariably, the sister would confirm that the baby was dead. She would then say, 'Let us put a screen around the bassinet. We will come back later and lay out the body.'

That harsh introduction to nursing made me question my strength and suitability for the profession, and I began to wonder if my father had not been right. I would think that perhaps Lenford Goniwe had been right, and his children were not meant to go into the nursing profession. After all, had he not vowed as much? However, as time went by, I observed the senior nurses and saw their genuine compassion towards the children in the ward. I also saw how their presence had a calming and reassuring effect on the little ones as well as their parents. I, too, began to relax and make the most of the guidance they offered us as we were learning our tasks. In time, I found that I was actually enjoying the experience, which helped me to gain confidence and assertiveness. Those were two traits that would stand me in great stead throughout my training.

Most of the children in Hut 2, the medical ward, were suffering from deficiency diseases such as kwashiorkor and anaemia, as well as gastroenteritis. The babies in the bassinets were succumbing to those diseases. That was my experience during the first three days of training. Poverty played a huge role in those diseases because the mothers could not afford a nutritious diet for their children. On admission days, the mothers would bring in the sick children, and the atmosphere in the ward would be tense. The children would be crying in pain or simply in solidarity with the other screaming children, while the mothers were anxious and concerned. We would have to screen the patients, separating those who would be admitted from those who simply needed to be processed through casualty. Then the serious work of processing the admissions would begin.

After the admission procedures had been completed, it would be a sad sight to watch a mother leave her baby behind for treatment. I learnt to respect the resilience of children as I watched them settle in after being separated from their loved ones and talk and smile with the nurses. I valued the experience that I gained in that ward. It groomed me and embedded in me a passion for women's and children's rights and the struggles of women the world over, which continue to inform my activism to this day.

Even during my husband's tours of duty in later years, it was rewarding to meet women from Malaysia and Canada, where he served, and to share with so many other spouses (mostly women, but there were also one or two men) about the conditions and struggles of women in the countries we came from.

After three months, the trial period was over, and the training programme for general nursing began. That was a hectic time. Even though the hospital was busy and we had to work hard, a monotony set in, and we were getting bored and anxious as exams were approaching. On one particular occasion, a month before writing the anatomy examination, we were making use of the lecture room, which was situated on the ground floor of the building.

To reach that room, one had to walk down a passage with a long wall. Along the wall were photos of all the nurses who had gone through the doors of that lecture room – all those who had studied nursing at King Edward VIII. Our lecturer was Miss Johnson, whom we loved, respected and feared at the same time. She was a tall woman, big and stout with an imposing and commanding forceful style.

The desks in the lecture room were arranged in straight lines with spacious aisles in between the rows that were wide enough to enable Miss Johnson to walk up and down. While seated there, we all faced the door to our right and a big white chalkboard, which occupied most of the top wall, in front. Sitting at our desks, we would recognise Miss Johnson's footsteps long before she entered the room. They were quick, brisk and heavy.

One particular day, we were sitting in the lecture hall and Miss Johnson had left us to our own devices as we prepared for the exam. It was sweltering, and it was after lunch, so we were all feeling tired. To avoid being inattentive, we decided to make use of the available teaching aids. The one that we agreed upon was a skeleton that hung, encased in a wooden box. I was one of the three trainee nurses who went to fetch it. To avoid breaking it while we wheeled it in and out of the classroom, we decided to remove it from the box and carry it and the empty box separately. First, the box would be wheeled to the lecture room. Then, the skeleton would be fetched and hung in its original position, ready for the demonstration.

The initial plan was that I would wheel the box to the lecture room, and the other two nurses would follow, carrying the skeleton. But we decided to jazz things up, instead. As soon as they took the skeleton out of the box, I jumped into it, and my colleagues quickly closed the door of the box and wheeled it into the lecture room with me inside, leaving the skeleton behind. It was an uncomfortable ride, and I was so afraid that if the box were to fall, I would be badly injured.

The wheels of the box I was in were rolling fast over the polished floor as it was being pushed to the lecture room. Once there, the box stopped abruptly in front of the waiting students. With a flourish, my fellow conspirators opened it and presented the teaching aid, me, whose anatomy was to be studied. They then started to point at different parts of my body, demanding that the fellow students in the lecture room name the anatomical parts they were pointing to. The class found the prank amusing and started laughing uncontrollably. During the raucous laughter, Miss Johnson came into the lecture room and wanted to know what was happening. It was difficult to stop laughing, but that proved convenient, as one could not laugh and answer the question at the same time.

So, there was no reply to Miss Johnson's questions. She gazed at us, puzzled, trying to figure out what was happening. Finally, she gave up and walked out of the room. Luckily, the matter ended there, and she never asked any more questions, which was just as well, since there would have been serious consequences had Miss Johnson found out what we had been up to.

Part 2

During

It was the best of times, it was the worst of times, it was the age of wisdom, it was the age of foolishness, it was the epoch of belief, it was the epoch of incredulity, it was the season of light, it was the season of darkness, it was the spring of hope, it was the winter of despair, we had everything before us, we had nothing before us, we were all going direct to Heaven, we were all going direct the other way ...

— **Charles Dickens: *A Tale of Two Cities***

When I first arrived in Pretoria in the mid-sixties, I found a community in limbo, awaiting imminent removal.

From early on in the 1950s, the community of Lady Selborne had lived with the knowledge that their township, my marital home, would be rezoned and become a white area. The legislation for the destruction of Lady Selborne had come into effect in 1958 and, in early 1962, the first removals had already taken place.

The 1962 removals had displaced some of the Lady Selborne community, including the Maganu and Mokae families, to Garankuwa. The Reverend Mokae and his wife were *abantu* – I only know the African sense of the word – and in that very humane sense of theirs, they looked out for us, even after *Doda* died and our family grew.

Garankuwa was a new township about 20 miles to the west of Lady Selborne. The Sesotho verb *goinkiwa* means 'to be taken'. Translated into English, the word *garankuwa* means that 'we have not been taken', so it is the antithesis of *goinkiwa*. No wonder that my father-in-law, *Doda*, felt that the name of that township, where the majority of its people had been forcibly removed from different locations to Pretoria, including Lady Selborne and Marabastadt, was a reflection of a truly ironic and abhorrent mind.

For those left behind in Lady Selborne, there was anxiety at the prospect of the imminent removal, which, for our family, happened in 1966. That was also the year of the birth of our first child. I had attended prenatal sessions at the clinic in Lady Selborne, which was run by Catholic nuns, and our first child, Susan, was born at the local hospital there, which was called the Little Flower. The celebration of her baptism was the last family function that we celebrated in Lady Selborne. The year 1966 was also the year in which Dimitri Tsafendas, a parliamentary messenger, stabbed and killed Hendrik Verwoerd in the apartheid parliament.

The 1960s were a time of turbulence. Indeed, British Prime Minister

Harold Macmillan made reference to 'the winds of change' that were blowing throughout the continent in his speech to Parliament in South Africa. In the 60s, seventeen African states were set to gain their independence. In South Africa, there was a veritable storm in progress. In contrast to the anticipated winds of freedom blowing in the countries to our north, here it was an ill wind that was blowing. The state's drastic measures taken to quell the storm simply served to stoke it more. That, despite the apartheid government declaring a state of emergency and later banning all political organisations, including the ANC and PAC.

Bizana, my home, and the whole of Mpondoland, were still in turmoil following the Mpondo Revolts, including the Nongquza Massacre and its aftermath. The eyes of the world, it seemed, were on Mpondoland, which had become the subject of a UN resolution in 1961 following the visit of UN Secretary-General Dag Hammarskjöld to South Africa. During that visit, he had met with the leaders of the Mpondo people in the Eastern Cape and reported on the situation there, which led to the UN Resolution.

Natal was in the throes of heightened political activity. In Pretoria, the Rivonia Treason Trial had been finalised in June 1964, and Mandela, Sisulu, Mlangeni and many of their peers were now on Robben Island serving life sentences.

The event that would shake South Africa to its roots and change the way the world viewed it was the Sharpeville Massacre. On 21 March 1960, the police had shot and killed 69 people and injured a further 186 who were protesting against the pass laws. On 30 March of that year, a state of emergency was declared.

In the townships, under the cloak of the State of Emergency, the police wreaked havoc by breaking into homes, arresting people and shooting at will those who were said to have 'tried to escape'. That triggered even more unrest, the most popularly known being the spontaneous march from Langa and Nyanga townships to the centre of town, led by Phillip Kgosana. Kgosana was a former Lady Selborne High School student, and he, Thomas Madumo, Joe Motsuga and my husband, Abe Nkomo, had been in the same 'dream' Form 1 class. All four were promoted from Form 1 to Form 3 and passed their Junior Certificate in the first class. All four were Africanists with PAC sympathies.

After his matric, all of the universities to which Kgosana had applied to study pharmacy rejected his application, informing him that Africans were not allowed to study pharmacy in South Africa. And so, he was persuaded by his brother to accept a South African Institute of Race Relations bursary to study economics and commerce at the University of Cape Town, instead. By 1960, Kgosana had joined the PAC, become its regional secretary for the Western Cape and abandoned his studies to become its full-time organiser.

As news spread of the predawn raids of 30 March, which had netted an estimated 2,000 arrests, Kgosana addressed a crowd of 5,000 daughters and sons of the soil in meetings at Langa, Nyanga and the Cape Flats. He also led a march of 30,000 to Parliament to press for the PAC demands, including the abolition of pass laws. The march was disciplined, but Kgosana and his delegation were duped into dispersing the crowd at the police station in Caledon.

Ignatius Terblanche, a senior police officer, promised Kgosana and his delegation a meeting with the Minister of Justice on condition that he ask the crowd to disperse. On Kgosana's orders, 30,000 demonstrators left peacefully and made their way home. When Kgosana and his delegation returned later for the meeting with the Minister of Justice, they were promptly arrested under the State of Emergency regulations.

The next day, police cordoned off Langa and Nyanga and proceeded to beat people and arrest them in house-to-house raids. That pattern of police action was repeated in townships across the country. By the second week of April, 20,000 people had been detained, and resistance began to peter out.

That was a difficult period. Nonetheless, following the 1961 Massacre, *Doda*, too, found himself forced into a mediation role between the people and an intransigent government. Fortunately, unlike Kgosana, he was not duped into detention – maybe because he had a much more prominent role internationally, thanks in part to his participation in the Moral Rearmament Movement.

In fact, my father-in-law, Dr W. F. Nkomo, was one of the leaders called upon to discuss the situation in South Africa at the time. He was also one of the leaders who discussed the political situation in South Africa with Dag Hammarskjöld during his visit to South Africa in 1961.

In the meantime, my application for admission to continue with midwifery training at King Edward VIII was accepted. I left the family, who were now beginning to settle into their new home in Atteridgeville and took my daughter to Bizana to be looked after by Mama while I joined my husband in Durban. He, too, was at King Edward, finalising his studies and beginning his housemanship.

꙲

In 1970, my husband Abe and I returned to Pretoria and began a new phase of our life of service. Abe worked with his father at his two practices in Atteridgeville and Saulsville, and we built our house in Saulsville at 43 Letlametlo Street. My husband's practice was right in front of our home. The address of the practice was 42 Loetse Street. We would live at 43 Letlametlo until 1985. It was a life filled with such beauty.

Doda was grateful for my husband's assistance, which left him free to pursue his other passions. He was an avid reader and lover of choral music. Among my most vivid memories are the choral music events he would host with the most exceptional choir being the one from the school of the blind, the Itireleng Mission.

I was to learn that the people of Pheli, Oustadt and Mzimdala (the old village) were rather snobbish. They looked down on the people from Saulsville. Atteridgeville and Saulsville are separated by one street, Sekhu Street. The houses to the west of Sekhu (towards Rustenburg) are in Saulsville, while those to the east towards town are in Atteridgeville. The Nguni schools, Bud-Mbele, Esikhisini and Makgatho, which my children could attend, were all in Saulsville. It seemed that Sotho (a Pretoria hybrid version) was the language of the people of Mzimdala. The rest of us, 'the others', who spoke Zulu, Xhosa, Shangaan, Venda, Ndebele, Swati and so on, mostly resided in Saulsville.

The hostel (*ihostela*) was in Saulsville, as were the places where one could buy *umqombothi*, or *mbamba,* a beer made from maize and sorghum. There was the home-brewed kind that was sold from the yard of the mama who made it, and there were the apartheid-approved beerhalls, which were always near the hostels. Those sold the boxed *mbamba*, proudly brewed by the National Sorghum Breweries (NSB) to keep the migrant workers 'heppi'. That also created executive committee jobs, which were fronts for their informers (*impimpi*) and increased the number of wealthy white entrepreneurs at the same time. Oh, the cunning of greed!

There were also a number of known shebeens in Saulsville that served Western alcohol. The third house opposite our home was one such shebeen. The couple who ran it had a daughter the same age as ours; her name was Louisa, and the two were friends. Not to be outdone, the third house in the same row as ourselves was also a shebeen. The proprietor of that one, known simply as Lily, was a local icon. The clientele of the shebeens were professionals like teachers and office administration workers.

In Saulsville, on the hill just in front of the hostel, there was an open space where, every Sunday, the men from the hostel would come out to perform traditional dances to the beat of drums. The drumming would go on incessantly as the hostel dwellers, joined by their peers from other hostels in the surrounding areas, would hold all kinds of events celebrating the various cultures that had been brought together by the migrant labour system.

In those days, you were more likely to see sangomas in their distinctive dress and African women clad in their *mitsheka* walking freely in Saulsville rather than in Atteridgeville. *Amapostela*, clad in their white and blue, would gather around open spaces, often near the train station in Saulsville, to hold their worship sessions. You would also see *iingamula yas'ehostela*. How my children loved watching the *ngamulas*; they never grew tired of it. An *ngamula* was a man who would dress up to the nines and stroll the streets. He would wear the most stylish, expensive-looking suits and hats, fedoras and the like. He would carry a walking stick, wear the most pristine white gloves and fashionable shoes, mostly two-tones; his shirt would be starched white, sometimes with frills, and sometimes, he wore bright suspenders holding up his pants – for aesthetic effect, not need.

Everything was about style. There would be bright ties, bow ties or even male neck bandanas matching the handkerchief in the breast pocket of the suit. There seemed to be polite competitiveness among the *ngamulas*, and the stakes were high: respect and serious bragging rights.

I cannot but smile every time I think of Ngoana Rakgadi. He had become an icon in the township. Initially, he had come from Malawi to work in the mines. With time, however, he had settled in here and provided an invaluable service to the community. Many of the families who lived around us were Christians and attended the local churches. However, many did not, and it was those people whom Ngoana Rakgadi serviced. When one among those people died, Ngoana Rakgadi would be there to preside over the ceremony, as well as the previous events, including the night vigil that was usually held the evening before the burial. In between those, Ngoana Rakgadi tended to do house visits in the neighbourhood. He would come into a home and offer a prayer for the family or the sick and infirm. Ngoana Rakgadi was always 'spic and span', which is to say tidily dressed in his white lab coat and white trousers and shiny black shoes. He carried a Bible in one hand and a silver bell in the other. If he were welcomed to bring his prayer into a home,

Ngoana Rakgadi would open the Bible to his chosen reading and ask if anyone wanted to read, hopefully, one of the children. What was remarkable is that while the appointed person was reading, invariably, Ngoana Rakgadi, who would also be reciting the verse, would surpass them. And throughout, Ngoana Rakgadi would be ringing the bell at what he considered significant parts. That was before performance religion and the advent of charismatic churches.

My husband's practice had grown very busy and, although officially he worked half days on Saturdays and Wednesdays and did not work on Sundays, in effect, he worked every day and most evenings. Then, after his official work time, we would go in to handle the dispensing. In those days, doctors like my husband were determined that their patients received the care and medicine they required, so they provided them with a consultation at a nominal fee with no cost for the medicine they prescribed. So, in most cases, Abe subsidised his patients' treatment, but even then, most of the patients were not in a position to pay for the services they received.

The extended working hours my husband kept often meant that planned family outings and visits had to be cancelled at the last minute. For example, the children would be all dressed up and ready to go to the Pretoria Show or the Rand Show, and then there would suddenly be a patient for Abe to see. He would open his practice and then one patient would become two patients and then three. By that time, the children would have realised what was happening and resigned themselves to another day at home. In that way, long-planned visits, such as those to the Pilanes in Saulspoort or the Molotlegis in Phokeng, would be suddenly cancelled.

There was also a protectiveness about the community of Saulsville. Generally, people knew each other and pooled together to assist when there were problems. There was a little girl called Minah who lived in the community. Minah, as people would say, was not well in her head: she had a mental disability. She was known by everyone, and her escapades would provide some amusement in the neighbourhood. But on one occasion, it ended tragically. For some reason, I do not think I ever knew why, Minah was agitated. She was walking along the road that passed our house, a main road of sorts, speaking loudly and pointing. People took her off the road and onto the pavement but, invariably, Minah would return to the road and continue with her angry rant. Again and again, she would be removed from the street but would then return. That went on until a car sped by and hit her. Right there on the street. The neighbours came running, calling the doctor and screaming, '*uMinah! Ushaise yi Moto*! (Minah has been hit by a car!)' We went out to find that Minah was dead.

When I think of that incident with Minah, I remember another occasion when our neighbours also intervened. Happily, the outcome of their intervention was a happy one. It involved our three boys, Phakamile, Gcobani and Woyisile, who were all young at the time – I think they were in preschool. Anyway, it was late one winter's afternoon, so it was already dark. My husband had parked his car outside the yard of his practice, behind which was our home. Three roads down, on the opposite side of the same road, was the Tshabalala home. Their house was quite distinctive because it had a long deep pool in front of it. That was because the son of that house, Joe, had converted to Islam, and we were told that the Muslim community in Laudium had built the pool so that they could perform Islamic rituals there.

Anyway, the boys spotted the car, and when they saw that the window of the driver's seat was open, they got inside, locked themselves in and started to 'drive' it. The car had a manual transmission, and they managed to engage the first gear. The neighbours saw the car moving off into the road, and they thought that it was heading towards the Tshabalala yard and pool. At that point, the boys were scared. They could not stop the car and were panicking. The neighbours physically held onto the car to stop it, while telling the boys to open the window so they could help them. But the boys were too panicked to respond appropriately. We heard the shouts from the street and ran out to find our car with the boys in it and several of our neighbours holding on to it for dear life. My husband managed to sprint to the car, open the door with the key and stop it. The boys, terrified and weeping, came out and ran home. Happily all had ended well.

Opposite the train station, there was a small market of vegetable and fruit vendors, which is where I used to shop. As a result, I had good relationships with most of the vendors and would generally stop to chat. They would enquire about my children, and I would ask about theirs. On one occasion, I was told by a vendor from whom I was buying about a horror that had happened to them. The vendor's little girl had been in hospital recovering from an attempted assault. She had been badly hurt, but to her mother's satisfaction, her daughter had bitten off the perpetrator's tongue. When they found her, she still had the tongue of the offender in her mouth.

At home, I was blessed with the assistance of Aunt Ida, whom I had inherited from *Doda* and *Mkhulu we Bhulu* (white). Aunt Ida had run *Doda's* home and now she lived with us. She was a wizard in the kitchen and could make all kinds of bread rolls and pies and cook up a storm. The kitchen was her domain, and even I was denied entry into it. Aunt Ida was also a staunch member of our church and a respected elder and would always return home with running commentary on the happenings there. Her position was always resolute, and she would pronounce it for all to hear. '*Ndabaxelela, basala bezinkukhu. Ndingu I. D. A. mna. Bazalisho balipele igama lam. I. D. A.* (I told them, and they were left speechless. They were like headless chickens. They would say my name and spell it as well. Me, I am I. D. A.).' Having grown up among storytellers, I thoroughly enjoyed I. D. A.

And then, *Makhulu we Bhulu* was different. Her focus was wholly on the children. She prided herself in having a clean and shiny environment around her. She loved tea, and her favourite variety was rooibos. *Makhulu we Bhulu*, as the children called her, was also *Makhulu we Planka*. She was *Makhulu we Bhulu* because she was very fair, almost Caucasian in appearance. She was *Makhulu we Planka* because she used the plank of a tomato box to instil discipline in the children. My children knew the feel of that tomato box plank keenly and became very disciplined, indeed.

To me, Saulsville was vibrant and alive. Atteridgeville, in contrast, was stiff, stylish in a Western kind of way and aspirant. The young people there were the '*klevas*', *tsotsis*, and those influenced by American Black Consciousness, with the urban (those in Atteridgeville) Africans mimicking African Americans who, in turn, were trying to imitate African style as a way of projecting their Black Consciousness. In Atteridgeville, they wore the *dashikis*, bold African prints, head wraps and big afros. They were the generation of Black Power. They were boys from the hood, *amakleva*. In their animated discussions, one would hear the phrase, '*Unyangidelela, ucabanga ukuthi ngiyibari yasemaplazini* (You disrespect me; you think I am a fool from the village).' Nonetheless, I appreciated the good jazz records they played and their jazz moves.

The older generation in Saulsville were more sedate. They were ardent churchgoers, and among them were the church leaders (*amagosa*), *amakhosikazi womanyano* (the women who held their prayer meetings on Thursdays in their distinct church uniforms) and the church choir. In the Methodist Church, where we worshipped, there were also the vibrant *amadodana ase Wesile* (the young men of the Wesley Methodist Church). We would all go to church on Sundays, and after the church service, the family would gather at *Doda's* house, 29/31 Nkosi Street. *Doda* presided over those gatherings. In the beginning, he had also attended the church services, but later, as his health deteriorated, he stayed at home. There, he would await our arrival after the service.

Doda would welcome us and, as the *makoti*, I and the daughters of the house would go into the kitchen to prepare lunch while *Doda* assembled his grandchildren around him. First, he would ask them about the church service. The grandchildren would then have to recount exactly what had happened in church, from the moment the service started until it ended. They would have to tell him which hymns were sung, which scriptures were read, who the preacher was and all about the sermon. Then, *Doda* would ask them about their week: what had happened during the week in school, how far they could count, the essays they might have written, their marks during a comprehension exercise, and so on. If *Doda* had travelled, he would tell them about his travels and, sometimes, he would give them gifts he had bought for them while he was away. After that, he would leave them to play and would then join the guests.

Sunday afternoons at *Doda's* house were quite an institution. When lunch was served, the platters would remain on the dining room table to be refilled constantly, as more guests came in throughout the day. After lunch, the gathering would move to the lounge, and the whole afternoon would be spent in discussion.

Those discussions ranged from local happenings and current affairs, articles in the local newspapers, *Doda's* concerns about the state of the community to the church or the happenings at Moral Rearmament. Sometimes, there would be just music – choral music – and debates about which choir was the best; sometimes there was poetry, and now and then, someone would play the piano with everyone else joining in to sing. We would leave the gathering in the early evening so that we could take the children home. We would also need to retire early, as we usually would have received guests the Saturday before. The main reason, however, was to enable *Doda* to continue holding court. And hold court he did.

A regular visitor to our house in Letlametlo Street in those days was our dear friend, George Molotlegi, who was also the younger brother of the King of the Bafokeng people, King Eddie Molotlegi. The children called him 'Uncle George'.

On most Saturday evenings, that dashing young man, dressed in the latest fashions out of *Ebony* and *Drum* magazines, would glide into our home, his ever-present entourage of changing faces in tow, and transform it into the most happening party in town. Other couples would join in, mostly friends we had made in Durban during the King Edward days. Those were long evenings of song and dance and laughter.

And then, the party ended.

Apartheid brutally separated families and friends and left us all incredulous, walking on eggshells and retreating into wells of silence. 'Fool said I, you do not know, silence like a cancer grows.' So go the words of a popular song by Simon and Garfunkel. George became estranged from us and from his family, as he aligned himself more and more with the Mangope regime and away from 'the people'. We saw less and less of him. When we did meet with him, it was no longer the same. As time went on, we settled into new norms. For our part, we as parents focused on the welfare of our children and the community they would grow up in.

However, the most shattering event, and the one that changed all of our lives, irrevocably, was the passing away of our beloved *Doda* in 1972. The world came to *Doda's* funeral, and so many tributes arrived as we mourned, which strengthened us and gave us the strength to continue with the task that he had left us. What was also helpful was that he had taught us well.

'Tribute to a Black Pilgrim' — Don Mattera

From your grave, a new message is born
That will echo through the corridors of time.
From the earth, a new race will issue forth,
Courageous, defying, daring and brimming
With ecstasy of new life and growth.
From your grave, a strong vision and dream
Will shape itself in reality –
That rise to take control over a dying land, strangled by Fear.
From your tears will come the balm to heal
Our shackled wrists and wounded spirits.
From the genitals of your loins,
A people loving freedom will proceed,
For you are Africa,
Its Blood, its Soul, its Soil,
Its Life, your sacred duty.
Its Blackness, your crowning beauty.

Then, a mere four years later, in 1976, our world turned on its head again.

The repression intensified. The events of 16 June 1976 in Soweto focused the world once again on South Africa and the brutality of the apartheid regime. We watched in horror as the violence spread across the country and, on 21 June, Atteridgeville was on fire.

It had started with the whisperings. The Sunday before, at church and everywhere you went, someone would pull you aside and ask, 'Did you hear? Tomorrow, Atteridgeville will strike.' So, later that Sunday, when my husband came across one of the teachers at our daughters' school, Teacher Gule, he asked him if he did not think it better that the little ones did not go to school the following day. Susan was ten years old and in Standard 3 at Makgatho Higher Primary School where Teacher Gule taught. But he assured my husband that nothing would happen, and we should not worry. He said, 'Everything is under control.'

On Monday morning, my husband drove Susan and the two Lusenga girls, who lived in the same street as us, to school. Mrs Lusenga, their mother, taught at Makgatho, so she went with them. On the way, the two adults devised a plan. Should anything happen, the girls were told to go to the church opposite the main entrance of the school and wait there until one of us came to fetch them. As it happened, after assembly when the children were in their classes, they could hear that something was happening outside in the courtyard. Older students, some from other schools, were conversing with the teachers and the principal in the school courtyard. They were also *toyi-toying* and making *Amandla* salutes.

And then, all hell broke lose. The police were there. They were telling the students to disperse and leave the school. Then there were shots and tear gas all over and a rain of stones, as students pelted the police vans. Dogs were unleashed and the Makgatho students were now also outside, and the teachers were trying to lead the younger girls and boys (Standard 3s) out through a back gate so they could get away from the chaos. The main gate, and thus the church Susan and her friends had been told to go to, was inaccessible. So the three girls joined their peers and Mrs Lusenga as they tried to walk home. They had to stop and try to hide and then run out again many times, evading tear gas and stones. Luckily, they made it safely back to to our house from where they tried to watch the havoc outside through the windows.

My husband and I had not been home at the time. When we heard what was happening, we dashed out to try and find the children. Having failed, we drove home, hoping to retrieve them along the way. What a relief it was to find them inside and safe. So we joined them, watching the happenings outside through the windows. At one point, we saw the neighbours running out of their homes towards a Boestra delivery van. The driver had abandoned it right in the middle of the road and its doors were all open. The neighbours were calling out to us, '*MaSuzi, MaSuzi, itla, go nal le borotho*! (Susan's mother, Susan's mother, come, there is bread!),' and then also '*Le di khekhe di teng*! ('There are also cakes!').' Some people were holding big basins full of bread and all kinds of baked delicacies from the van. And then, pandemonium: the police arrived with tear gas and dogs. The people tried to escape. Some abandoned the purloined goods; others managed to hold on to their bread. The dogs were let loose among them and tear gas filled the air. There were bread and buns scattered all over the street.

A while later, as we continued to watch, we heard the children, who were pointing to Teacher Gule. He was running down the road with others, fleeing a police van that was firing rubber bullets and throwing out tear gas canisters. The children in the house were pointing at him and screaming, 'Everything is under control; everything is under control!' I am sad to say that, from then on, we referred to Teacher Gule as 'Everything is under control'.

The violence was indiscriminate. As the days went by, the township had become a war zone, and the military had moved in. Every day, their Hippos drove up and down the streets. Whenever more than two people were together in public, they were considered to be a gathering. Three people walking down a street constituted an illegal gathering, and teargas could be thrown at them to disperse them. At night, those soldiers and the Special Branch police would conduct house-to-house raids in the township. During those raids, the beatings were indiscriminate. Schooling had stopped. The medical practice was receiving scores of people who had been beaten up and badly injured by the police. The bodies started piling up, and funerals became battle zones.

Whenever there was a funeral for a person who had been killed by the regime, the police would guard that home, harassing and, at times, sending away those who were coming to commiserate with the bereaved family. On the day of the funeral, police would be there to terrorise the family and cause general discord. One of their favourite actions during such a funeral was to form a semicircle in front of the cemetery gate, standing ready with sjamboks in hand. They would tell the mourners that only close members of the family were allowed into the cemetery and therefore to the graveside to bury the deceased. That desecration of a funeral, right next to the person's final resting place, was seen as the ultimate violation.

Most of the time, that would lead to a confrontation and conflict. The vicious circle would start again, and people would be beaten up or shot. When an injured person was taken to the hospital, there would be a policeman waiting to arrest them and place them under 24-hour police guard. It was quite 'normal' for someone who had gone to a funeral to end up alone and in pain in a hospital and to die with only the police guard present.

If someone from the group attending the funeral died, the macabre ritual would start all over again. At such a funeral, the agents of the state, *impimpi*, would come back with a vengeance, targeting the mourners in church, noting what was said and who had said it. They would point out the 'agitators' among the mourners to the Special Branch police, and such people would be arrested – sometimes, right there at the funeral. From our perspective, an agitator would be any community leader who aligned themselves with the people or anyone who simply spoke out against injustice and was therefore trusted in the community. Father Tsebe, the local priest of the Anglican Church and a beloved member of the community, was fingered as an agitator; Mrs Rosina Mphahlele was fingered as an agitator, and so too was my husband, Abe Nkomo. At the same time, so many of our young people, school children really, were being vilified and labelled agents provocuteur. Like the Masuku brothers, our girls and boys were being turned into orphans and fugitives or being forced into exile, arrested or simply being disappeared, never to be heard of again.

There was no respect for the sanctity of burial sites. At some funerals, the mourners and the priest would be compelled to abandon the coffin at the gravesite, fleeing tear gas fumes and rubber bullets. The police would also wreak havoc at the home of the bereaved where burial society members comprising neighbours and friends would be cooking for the mourners. Those caterers would be assailed with teargas and forced to flee, leaving scattered pots, the contents of which would have spilled out and been left to burn on the open fires.

No place was safe. Mitta Ngobeni was three years old when she was shot dead while playing in the yard of her home. Three years old. Shot in the head and left there to die. Her brain was scattered on the ground.

The police also engaged in a concerted campaign to divide the community. Every institution in the community was affected. Even the church was not spared. In our church, respected church elders in service of the regime stood up and labelled congregants, including my husband, as instigators who were responsible for influencing students to revolt against the government. The congregants, themselves members of the community and thus witness to the atrocities perpetrated by the members of the police and the army, would sit in silence while the collaborators stood on the pulpit berating my husband and other community leaders, including the priests. It was rule by fear.

In the midst of all that, our house would be petrol bombed one day, my husband's practice the next day, and then the house would be bombed once more, and then again, the practice. When the practice had been repaired, sometimes with the help of friends and colleagues such as Dr Ribeiro, the police would ensure that no patients would be able to come in. A police car would park outside the whole day, intimidating people who wanted to consult with the doctor. Sometimes, a patient would find themselves confronted by a police officer, notebook in hand, demanding that they provide their name and address.

We continued as best we could, under the circumstances. Most consultations had to be done as house calls or, in some cases, the patients would come to our home for a consultation. In the midst of all that, however, there would be amazing incidents that would lift our spirits and leave us in awe.

Once on a Sunday evening, while we were still living in Saulsville, a young man was brought into the house. His arm was bleeding profusely from a bullet wound, but he was beaming: he had the biggest, brightest smile. In his other hand, he was holding the key to a Casspir, the property of the South African Army.

According to him, he had passed the scene of a heated altercation between members of the community and a group of army boys who had been the occupants of the Casspir, the key of which he was now carrying. According to him, amazingly, the soldiers had left the Casspir unattended with the key in the ignition. When he passed by the soldiers, they were so absorbed in their altercation with members of the community that they had not seen him approach the Casspir. That young man had simply reached into the driver's side of the vehicle and taken the key out. I am not sure how it came about that the soldiers finally realised what was happening, or how he came to be shot, but there he was, key in hand and with only a minor wound. The soldiers had been left stranded in the street.

Other areas were not fairing any better. The South African townships had become killing fields, and we were all caught up in it. The killing fields extended into the police stations and police cells. In 1977, the police killed Stephen Bantu Biko in Pretoria while he was in detention. That incident was particularly shattering to us. We learnt of the atrocious conditions under which he had been held and the way it was claimed he had died. At the time, it was reported in the media that he was the twelfth person to have died in police detention during the twelve months between 1976 and 1977.

In 1979, Solomon Kalushi Mahlangu was hanged, becoming one of the 139 political prisoners the apartheid government killed in that way between the 1960s and 6 June 1995, when capital punishment was abolished in South Africa.

We were still counting the bodies. The roll call was increasing.

Griffiths Mxenge was killed in 1981, and four years later, his wife Victoria Mxenge was hacked to death in their home in front of their children. Victoria and I had trained together in midwifery at King Edward.

The number of threatening anonymous phone calls increased, and the familiar disembodied voice would ask me, 'Did you see what happened? Have you bought flowers for your husband's coffin yet?' Then the house would be bombed again. My husband's practice would be bombed again.

We survived, in large part, because of our neighbours, who had learnt to be vigilant. Ever ready with water to douse the fire; ever ready to raise the alarm whenever a suspicious car, often without number plates, occupied by white men with army-cut hair and sometimes accompanied by known Special Branch police, was sighted. At those times, there would be heightened vigilance in the homes of the activists. But there is no amount of vigilance that can secure an entire community against the concerted efforts of Pretoria's Covert Operation Units. We would wake up to reports about which home had been raided, who had been arrested, who had managed to evade arrest and whether anyone had tried to approach our home or my husband's practice.

The covert operations were not only carried out by known government officials, there were members of the community who openly colluded with the government. Once, a very well-known businessman, whose business was struggling, tried a false trick on my family. That man went to my husband's practice and told him that he had heard from reliable sources that he and my husband would be arrested that night. He encouraged my husband to skip the border, suggesting that he go to Botswana. He even suggested the border post that Abe should use. My husband thanked Mr 'X' for the information and advice. After that, he came home to confer with the family. The consensus was that he was going nowhere. As a result of that false information, I destroyed valuable books and important documents, just in case the expected visitors did not approve of them. But that night, the expected visitors did not arrive.

We were thankful that the night had passed without incident. We were also pleased that we had not yielded to the lies Mr 'X' was spreading. At least, this one time, a family had been left intact. We knew so many who had followed the advice of those so-called saviours only to be abducted and killed or made to flip to the other side.

Later, the following evening, Mr 'X's car was seen parked near my husband's practice. He seemed to be checking to see if my husband was there. I am sure he was disappointed that Abe had not left the country and attempted to go into exile as he had been advised to. There was never a reference to his lies, and every time we met, it was as if the incident had never happened. One would have thought that it had occurred in a dream, were it not for the ashes of our books I had burnt. They were the only evidence that the incident had taken place.

Life went on.

꒳

One of my passions has always been cooking, which is something I shared with many of my friends, so a group of us registered for culinary school. That was fun. I also registered with Unisa for a BCur Nursing, majoring in Community Health Nursing and Nursing Administration. I then went to England to study for an M.Phil. in Community-based Disability Studies at the University of London. After that, I went to work at the Medicos Special School in Soshanguve.

So much was disruptive. Schooling was intermittent; many young people were trying to leave the township, some succeeding and others being arrested or killed in the attempt. Some left to join relatives in the Bantustans to continue their education. Families were being broken apart and, as a result, many of the aged were effectively abandoned and needed care. People came together to address that crisis, and the Atteridgeville\Saulsville branch of the Society for the Care of the Aged was formed. Local social workers were the driving force of the organisation, and when they approached me, I volunteered to do administrative work for the Society.

Membership of the Society for the Care of the Aged consisted of the recipients of old-age grants. Committee members were elected from the general membership of the organisation with the guidance of the social workers and were allowed to co-opt members from the community onto the board. In that way, I found myself elected as Secretary of the Society for the Care of the Aged, in my early thirties.

Back then, the Society for the Care of the Aged was very active. Their activities centred around the one or two pension collection days per month. On those days, the Society had to be especially vigilant, as the collection points would be very busy and traders would try to take advantage of the pensioners. Non-governmental organisations (NGOs) also assisted, such as the Salvation Army, who provided soup and bread for them.

The committee would also initiate activities in the community at the behest of the pensioners. For example, on the recommendation of the Society, the committee invited Bishop Barnabas Lekganyana of the Zion Christian Church (ZCC) to visit the communities of Atteridgeville and Saulsville. There was such excitement in anticipation of that visit. The day before the Bishop's address, members of the ZCC arrived by train and bus from all the surrounding townships and even further. That initiative of the Society for the Care of the Aged brought out most of the organisations in the community. One in particular stood out: the Society for a Creative Community. Two of its leaders deserve special mention: Mrs Rosina Mphahlele and Mrs Dora Nkamane. The Society for a Creative Community united people around a campaign against a growing practice of that time: ostentatious spending at funerals. The campaign found resonance and was widely supported.

Mrs Dora Nkamane had been an educationalist for a long time, and even when school attendance was disrupted in the township, she worked hard as the coordinator of the Pretoria branch of the Sached Trust to assist students to qualify for and write their matric under trying conditions and then to win bursaries to enable them to further their education.

Mrs Rosina Mphahlele was a passionate champion of the rights of people with disabilities. In particular, she was concerned about children with disabilities and their ability to access education. While those organisations were becoming more prominent in the township, so too was the work of the Residents' Organisation, which was increasing its campaigns against the illegitimate local authorities and the police. I believe that those intergenerational links within the organisations in our area were quite unique, which explained why those who collaborated with the regime would single out the leaders of those organisations and accuse them of instigating young people against the system. That was ironic because, although most of the youth in our township were radicalised, it was caused by the conduct of the regime – more specifically, the police.

As Oupa Masuku was to testify to the Truth and Reconciliation Commission years later, he was thirteen years old in 1977 when he was arrested for the first time under Section 22 of the Terrorism Act. Although those charges were dropped, there were many other charges later, and he was not the only one. It was striking to me that young people in Atteridgeville knew the police from Compol and the Pretoria region, including the Atteridgeville police, by name. There was a cynical overfamiliarity between the gun and its target: a perverse dance of wounding and staying in focus before the kill.

That student crisis concerned the residents deeply, and in those years, members of the Residents' Organisation were working with the students and bringing in leaders from other communities, including Dr Nthato Motlana, himself a leader of a residents' organisation, and Archbishop Desmond Tutu to assist in addressing those problems. That was even before the launch of the United Democratic Front (UDF) in August 1983.

At one o'clock in the morning on 5 March 1985, the Masuku home in Atteridgeville was bombed. Madiphoso Masuku was killed, and the eldest of her four sons, Ezekiel 'Oupa' Masuku, was badly injured. In a cruel irony, the Special Branch police, who were implicated in that event, claimed that Mrs Masuku's sons had bombed their home and killed their mother. That was bad enough, but what was to follow was truly horrifying. We were witness to those events, about which Oupa would later testify.

Oupa was injured on Tuesday 5 March but only discharged from the hospital on the 8th, the day before his mother's funeral, which was to be held on Saturday the 9th. A few hours after he had returned home, the police arrived with a court order restricting the number of people who could attend the night vigil. They had erected roadblocks at all the entrances to Atteridgeville, and they had also brought in reinforcements from Soshanguve so that the whole evening before the funeral, people who were trying to attend were threatened, intimidated and, in some cases, beaten up. All that was arbitrary: we do not count the number of mourners who attend a vigil or the people who congregate at the home of the bereaved. By the time I got home from the hospital, people had already converged at the house, and I was told that many were still trying to come, despite the police squadron around our home and at the entrances of the township.

The police returned that same night with a second court order: this time, restricting the number of people who were allowed to attend the funeral the next day. On the day of the funeral, the police were at it again. They actually escorted the hearse from the church to the graveyard, all the time harassing the family and the mourners, even pointing guns at them from the Casspirs. They were particularly aggressive towards those mourners who were wearing t-shirts bearing the face of the deceased, which had been organised by the community. At the cemetery, the police blocked the entrance, restricting the number of people who could enter. Those who were allowed to go in proceeded with the graveside part of the burial process and returned home. There, too, the police arrived and sprayed a purple substance at the tent where the people were gathering. They also attacked the people who had gathered at the house, beating everyone, young and old, women and children, and injuring them – some were left paralysed. A lot of damage was done to the house.

Many people were concerned about the safety of the now doubly orphaned Masuku boys who, after being encouraged that they would be safer outside Atteridgeville, quietly left their home in the chaos. The house was left abandoned for a while. The situation was becoming dire throughout the township, and most of the comrades had been warned not to sleep at home. Many of the young activists volunteered to spend the nights at our home to keep watch. On one occasion, while they were keeping watch, some patrolling at various points outside, they saw police vans approaching the house. Suddenly, armed policemen jumped out of the vans and scaled the fence. The comrades ran into the house to warn us, and just then, there was a knock at the front door. The loud knock we were so familiar with. As we were attending to that, the comrades who had run into the house decided to lie down in the rooms, all of them covered by blankets. Some were sleeping on beds, but most were lying on the floor.

One of the policemen remarked, 'I see you have a big family.' Some of his colleagues laughed. I thought that perhaps they were just there to intimidate us: to let us know that they were aware of our novice attempts at erecting a security system of sorts and that they found it laughable. But it became immediately clear that they had a different purpose in mind when they started ransacking the house. They searched every nook and cranny, and this time, the search was frantic: they were definitely looking for something and were convinced that they were going to find it. They were turning everything over, throwing everything out, including the contents of the wardrobes. They even opened the cisterns. They threw the books from the bookshelves, ignoring incriminating books, so they certainly were not looking for documents but hardware. When they were satisfied that whatever they were looking for was not there, they left, again commenting on the large size of the family. A clear reference that they had not been fooled about who the people were who had been covered under the blankets.

On the night he was detained, my husband Abe had just arrived home from doing house calls. Our youngest son, Marumo, who was a toddler then, was still awake as he had sat up with me, waiting for his father to return. There was a knock at the door. When I peeped through the window, I saw members of the Special Branch standing in pairs, lined up from the gate all the way to the front door There were also female members wearing nice navy blue suits and boots. With them was a Black gentleman in civilian clothes. He avoided eye contact.

This time, the police stated the purpose of their visit. They told us that they were there to detain my husband. It was a very cold July evening, and it struck me that they had bothered to advise him to dress warmly. After that, one of the policemen literally tailed my husband as he went about collecting what he thought he would need. Marumo also went along with his father. When I asked where they were taking my husband, they said the Wierdabrug Police Station and put him into a police van. We had accompanied my husband to the gate, in front of which were several police vehicles. There was also an open van with barking dogs. When Marumo saw that, he started crying and asked, 'Mama, where are they taking Daddy?'

I remember trying to hold him and console him, but the next thing I knew, he had run off and was trying to chase after the convoy of cars that were taking his father away. He ran right to the end of the road, calling after his father.

We started the process of going to find the prison the very next day. It turned out that my husband was not at the prison I had been told to go to. Eventually, I was informed that he was at a police station in Lyttelton, where we finally found him. We found out that a lot of activists from Atteridgeville and the surrounding townships had also been detained: Ronnie Mamoepa; the Legoro brothers, Mpho and Nathaniel; Titus Mafolo; Ata Mkhwanazi; Reeves Mabitisi; Mathew Sathekge; Ramie Dau; Father Mkhatshwa; Sandy Lebese; Jackie Masemola; Reverend Hlaletwa; Stanza Bopape and many others. They were subsequently all moved to 'New Lock' where they were kept for more than a year. Even Oupa Masuku, who had lost his mother barely three months earlier and was still nursing the wounds he had sustained in that incident, was detained while attending an enquiry into her death. Right there at the inquest, Oupa was arrested, taken to Compol and then to the same facility as my husband and the others.

We found a way of continuing, somehow, but it was becoming difficult. Nolitha was at St Mary's DSG. Three of the boys, Phakamile, Gcobani and Woyisile were at St Albans, while Marumo was at Waterkloof Higher Preparatory School (WHPS). Those were all in Pretoria East. I worked at Medunsa, which was in Pretoria North. Abe had been mostly responsible for the school shuttling, which now I had to find a way to manage. There were amazing guardian angels who stepped forward to assist. Meryl Horn and Mary Anne McRobert immediately offered to shorten the journey by meeting me on the way every morning and dropping the children at their various schools. Later, we came up with the more practical arrangement of leaving the children with Mary Anne McRobert during the week and only picking them up for weekends.

Marumo was too young for that, as he had just started Grade R at WHPS. Thankfully, the Reverend Peter Beukes and his wife Isobel offered to help us. They lived in Atteridgeville where Peter was the priest in the Anglican Church, having moved there after the death of Father Tsebe. Michael, their youngest son, was the same age as Marumo and also went to WHPS. So Isobel did most of the taxiing for Marumo and Michael. In time, we fell into a routine that enabled the children's schooling to proceed, unencumbered, while also allowing me to continue at Medicos.

Our immediate rescuers to run the practice after the detention were Roy and Marjorie Jobson. We met them after they had just returned from then-Venda where they had both worked after Roy's graduation until their return to Pretoria. They had been employed at the Donald Fraser Hospital at Vhufuli, which was a hospital that Roy's grandfather, Douglas Aitken, had built in 1933. Both Roy's grandfather and his wife Irene had served at that hospital for 35 years. The conditions under which Roy had served there sounded challenging. Their stories of Vhufudi made me think so much of Bizana and wish that there had been a similar health care institution there. Marjorie told me that when they had gone to Venda, their first child, Geoffrey, was only two weeks old.

Roy was mostly alone in a 400-bed hospital with 21 outlying clinics and

200 outpatients a day – an impossible demand on any human being – but he loved it and got to know every nurse. I was also struck by Marjorie's description about the help she had received from the nurses. They had assisted with interpretation and taking care of Geoffrey – with Sister Vera Tshivase going as far as strapping him on her back to free Marjorie, herself a medical doctor, to be able to help with the outpatients.

Upon their return to Pretoria in 1985, Marjorie worked at Kalafong hospital. She was a member of the Black Sash and, as part of her work, she was involved with the Emergency Services Group of doctors who provided assistance to detainees and others. The group also produced a booklet, *Coping in Crisis*, which, at that very dangerous time, carried Marjorie and Roy's home phone number as the contact for those in need. After the swoop by the security police at the beginning of the State of Emergency, Marjorie found that most of her colleagues were in detention, such as Anneke, who had been detained, put in solitary confinement and then immediately deported to Sweden: straight out of prison and onto a plane.

Our other rescuers, who immediately came in to assist and provide relief to the Jobsons, were three young doctors: Dr Paul Sefularo, Dr Racks Ledwaba and Dr Steven Komati. Dr Confidence Moloko had secured that team and coordinated with them to run the practice. It was quite an enterprise. Just two weeks before my husband was detained, his surgery was bombed again for the umpteenth time. We had barely finished repairing it from the previous attack. As mentioned, for over a year the police had been intimidating us, trying to stop patients from entering the practice by parking outside, day in and day out, and noting who came in. That had harmed the practice.

I am eternally grateful to those doctors who took up the responsibility of running and managing the practice, unremunerated and exposing themselves and possibly their families to immense danger. That restored my faith in the essential goodness of the human soul. But what they were attempting was really a holding operation, as the practice generated just enough to keep going. That is, the doctors could pay the support staff and buy the medicine they were dispensing at the practice, but that was all. We could derive nothing from it, financially, but we were determined to keep it going. For us, that was an important statement of defiance and solidarity. Attempts to lure us into 'exile' and possibly death or disappearance, bombings, death threats and intimidation campaigns had all failed to stop the practice. Now, detention would also fail to do so.

By the end of the year, the situation was ominous. After what had been a concerted campaign of continuous bombings of our home and medical practices, as well as the virtual free practice we were compelled to run, there were serious financial challenges. Each time after a bombing, we had to make repairs to the home or the practice. In the case of the practice, we had to replace the merchandise, and when Abe was detained, we were already struggling. What I was earning from Medunsa hardly paid for my trips to work and back. The children had to be fed – there were so many expenses and no sign of a reprieve. My biggest worry was the school fees. I was at my wits' end. I had to find money for the school fees. This time, our guardian angel was my sister-in-law, Punie, who was the wife of Abe's younger brother, Kali Nkomo. Punie was working for Johnson & Johnson at the time. Aware of the strain I was under, Punie had outlined the challenge of the school fees to her employers, and Johnson & Johnson had kindly offered to relieve me of that burden. They paid the fees.

There were also good friends who would step in and brighten a day, a week or a whole month. The Pilanes and the Molotlegis ensured that, during that first December, we had sufficient meat and vegetables. They would send vegetables and a slaughtered sheep and chickens. It looked like even if the children did not have their father through the holidays, especially Christmas, we could at least make sure they were well fed.

Thankfully, on occasion, there would be enough from those gifts left to share with some of the other mothers who were in the same situation as ours. One Sunday in December, I think it must have been before Christmas, but I am not too sure, a group of men came to the house and announced that they were there to sing for us. It was an *isicathamiya* group (Zulu singing style similar to a capella). I cannot remember what the group was called, but they brought us such joy. The children loved them. All that December, I would hear singing 'Oh, my chicken roasting in the oven, my chocolate, my … ' But it was clear: their father was not coming home for Christmas.

The detainees were allowed one visit every two weeks, and each time, we had to present ourselves at the prison administration offices to obtain permission to visit, which was clearly designed to humiliate and frustrate us and perhaps even discourage us from visiting the detainees. I cannot explain the humiliation we experienced at the hands of the foolish young white girls who attended to us. When I informed Meryl and Maryanne about what had occurred on those occasions, they immediately volunteered to accompany me whenever I went there, and they did.

In their presence, our reception was more cordial, or at least the foolish young white girls who attended to us seemed less inclined to humiliate us in the presence of the older white women. When accompanied, I was Mrs Nkomo. On those days, I had magically acquired some respectability. I was suddenly not the 'girl' they had made fun of in various ways, like mocking my first name: 'Wat? Magarien? Majo-rie, Ma wat?' Now, I was Mrs Nkomo in front of Mrs McRobert and Mrs Horn. What I am grateful to those lasses for, however, is that after that, I can now say that I love my other name, Marjorie. It is no longer just a functional name, it is now a name I claim proudly, just like Nomasomali. It was also interesting to see that those young ladies were embarrassed by what they were doing in the service of officialdom and, in front of their people, they had been forced to behave differently.

At home, life resembled a game of musical chairs. The mostly male activists who had occupied the dining table in my home, holding ad hoc meetings, mainly about the issues and challenges facing the Atteridgeville/Saulsville Residents' Organisation (ASRO), were now all in detention. The irony was not lost on me that they had been replaced by our team of women. On many occasions, our meetings would go on late into the night as the wives of the other detainees and I discussed our common challenges and explored possible solutions. We would also get input from allies who were working on those within the Nats to find out what was likely to happen next and when the release of detainees might take place.

We were strengthened by the gestures of support we were receiving. My husband had been a lay preacher of the Methodist Church and had been participating in its national structures. One of the victories that they, as the Black Caucus, were celebrating was the installation of its first African president, Bishop Stanley Mogoba. After so much persistence and activism, they had finally succeeded. I was excited to receive Bishop Mogoba at our home. He had just returned from a conference of the World Council of Churches (WCC).

During his visit, Bishop Mogoba told me that he was on a mission to our house, having been sent by the Council. The delegates of the WCC had taken note of the situation in South Africa and had made important resolutions during the conference, which he had come to share with us. But what saddened me was that to bring that message of support to us, the Bishop had gone to great lengths to ensure that he was not seen entering our home.

When I walked him out of the house, I saw that he had not parked his car outside of our home but several streets away, in front of a shopping complex, so that no one would know that he had come to see us.

The esteemed Bishop was not the only one who had felt that they had to hide when conveying their support. In the case of Mrs Domingo, I was very touched and heartened, as she went to great lengths to slip into our home, unobserved, just to be with us and maybe share a prayer, even though she believed that by doing so, she was risking her pension. Mrs Domingo was a widowed pensioner. Her husband had been a policeman and therefore she was dependant on her pension from the state. She was a dear woman who was appalled by what was happening to us and would phone and ask that we leave the back gate open so that she could slip into the house unobserved. I was always touched that she made a point of leaving us some money – R100 on one occasion, R200 on another, saying that we must get something for the children.

We also received a visit from Paul Veryn and messages from *Oom* Bey (Beyers Naude) as well as Archbishop Desmond Tutu. Beyers Naude and Archbishop Tutu served on the Board of Kagiso Trust with my husband, Dr Abe Nkomo.

The extent of the repression and the violence unleashed resulted in a flurry of non-governmental organisations becoming active in Atteridgeville. In addition to the assistance they gave us in highlighting the situation of the detainees held under the State of Emergency and the challenges we faced, those NGOs found themselves compelled to address the challenges that had led to the protests in the first place. They conducted law clinics in the community and were amazed at the level of organisation and community-based initiatives taking place in Atteridgeville. In particular, Marjorie Jobson and, prior to her deportation, Anneke van Gijlswyk were constant allies.

An unexpected ally emerged in the form of a strong contingent of women associated with the National Party (NP) who were quite influential in its circles. Included were two formidable women, Martie-Meiring and Ora Joubert, who brought in people like Rina Venter, the NP Minister of Welfare, to see for themselves the havoc wrought by the police and occupying army in our midst – in particular, the killing of Mrs Madipholo Masuku and the fate of her sons. They were horrified, had many questions and were determined to get answers.

That, in itself, was indicative of the tensions that were intensifying within the ruling party. Until then, it had been the Black Sash who had mostly been present – along with the ebullient Anneke van Gijlswyk, Marjorie Jobson and the disparate team of women they sometimes brought with them, some of whom were members of the Pretoria chapter of the Black Sash.

Anneke and Marjorie had served with my husband on the Pretoria Crisis Committee, and it was they who had approached ASRO with their appeal for assistance with the problem of the compulsory conscription of young white boys into the Army. Conscription was having a terrible impact on them: they had participated in horrific unmentionable acts in the townships and in the frontline states and were now acting out at home. Their mothers were desperate and had no way of helping to facilitate the rehabilitation processes that were clearly necessary. The ASRO Executive referred the matter to us, the ASRO women's committee and, immediately, Mrs Rosina Mphahlele took leadership, working with the local team of families of the detainees and those who had lost loved ones at the hands of the army, including the mother of Mitta Ngobeni and the Masuku family.

In Mamelodi, similar meetings were taking place. Marjorie was also working with the Khulumani Support Group and, within the auspices of Khulumani, the Khulumani Mothers of the Disappeared, a group of 21 mothers whose sons had been disappeared and eliminated.

By June 1986, my husband had been in detention for more than a year. I had grown used to not knowing what to expect next and had been reflecting on that during a weekend when Susan had come to visit. She had gone back to campus on Sunday. On Tuesday morning, as I was preparing to go to work, I got a call asking me if I was aware that another state of emergency had been declared the night before and that many arrests had been made. At the time, I had not heard anything. When I arrived at Medicos for work, I was told that there had been a call for me. My daughter had been detained under the State of Emergency.

Susan and her friend, Thandi Gqubule, were taken together from Jubilee Hall, the residence where they stayed, to John Vorster Square and held in solitary confinement. I went to John Vorster Square but was not allowed to see Susan. I spent that whole day trying to get information, during which I met with Reverend Gqubule and his wife, who were Thandeka's parents, and Mama Albertina Sisulu, whose son Zwelakhe had also been detained the night before. It seemed that he had been brought in at the same time as Raymond Suttner.

Two months later, Thandeka Gqubule's parents and I were granted permission to visit the girls for the first time, on the same day. The Gqubules had travelled from their home in Pietermaritzburg to see their daughter. By that time, Susan and Thandeka had been moved to 'Sun City' (Johannesburg

Prison) in Soweto. As mentioned, we had not been granted permission to see them at John Vorster Square.

I met Reverend and Mrs Gqubule at the prison gate, and we entered the prison together. At reception, the Gqubules and I introduced ourselves and identified the detainees we had come to see.

We had to wait for the girls to be brought in. After a while, we were escorted to two separate cubicles next to each other in a row of similar cubicles. While I was waiting on my side of the cubicle, the grate on the other side opened and Susan walked in and sat down opposite me. We were separated by a wall and glass. Susan insisted that she was well and wanted to know how everyone else was: her father, her siblings and me.

She wanted me to tell everyone that she was well. The visit was short. It was winter, and I had brought in some warm clothing, including a pair of ankle-length boots. She was so happy about that humble offering and that the prison had accepted them and would pass them on to her later. I was pleased she could have them. She told me that at John Vorster Square she got so cold that she would lean against the wall where there was a thin hot water pipe. As a result, she had a dark line across her lower back where the pipe had burnt into her skin. Luckily, that ugly scar had not become infected, even though it had caused her some discomfort.

Visit over and very relieved, I joined the Gqubules outside the cubicles as we exchanged details and prayed together in thanksgiving. We held together in prayer in a prison, grateful that our girls were there and that the Lord had kept them. It was not a little thing this one: we were aware of so many others who had not been as fortunate. We were truly blessed. I then had to go back to Pretoria to tell Susan's anxious siblings that I had been able to see her and get permission to see Abe and tell him that she was well – or at least as well as one could be after two months of solitary confinement at John Vorster Square.

Although I tried to get permission to see Susan again, I only got to see her that one time at Sun City. Luckily, however, the pressure mounted and, at the insistence of Judge Goldstone, Susan was released two months later. She was glad to be out but sad to have left her friends behind, especially Thandeka. We managed to get Susan a visit to see her father for the first time after her release from Sun City. Then we fitted ourselves back to surviving, as we had done before.

Susan returned to Wits and managed to attend the UN Conference in Harare. She was the student representative in the Federation of Transvaal

Women (FEDTRAW) and, on occasion, she would come home with Thula Ngcobo, the rep from Medunsa; Gugu, who represented students in the Natal Organisation of Women (NOW), and Nomboniso Gasa, who represented students in the United Women's Congress (UWCO).

At the same time, more activities were being spurred on by the UDF, a concerted effort was being made to render the country under apartheid ungovernable, and the activities of the End Conscription Campaign were gaining momentum. A delegation of white intellectuals went to meet with representatives of the ANC in Senegal. It was now increasingly the members of the establishment and no longer just the white left and the religious sector who were questioning the National Party and apartheid brutality. At stake were no longer just the atrocities against Black people in the townships and the frontline states, but young white men as well.

By the time the detainees returned, the first signs of the rupture in the National Party were becoming more and more apparent as the voices of the decent surfaced from within it. There were signs that P. W. Botha, *Die Groot Krokodil*, was losing his grip and becoming increasingly isolated within his party. Members of the NP were making overtures to the leadership of the banned organisations in exile, and there was a confrontation between the securocrats and those who wanted to present a more enlightened, forward-looking plan.

The centre was no longer holding.

ॐ

The first of the Rivonia Trialists to be released was Govan Mbeki. Then, in October 1989, Walter Sisulu, Elias Motsoaledi and Andrew Mlangeni were released. There was excitement as Sisulu was scheduled to land at Jan Smuts Airport, and Susan was among the Wits students who went to welcome him there. The violence that met the jubilant crowd assembled to welcome Tat'uSisulu was an important reminder that Pretoria was grudgingly giving in to the inevitable. Indeed, throughout the transition process, the violence would continue, in various forms, right up until 1994. In fact, in June 1992, Nelson Mandela halted the negotiations until September, following the Boipatong Massacre, where more than 40 people were killed with knives, guns and axes. In April 1993, Chris Hani was killed.

On 2 February 1990, F. W. de Klerk announced the unbanning of all political organisations and the release of Tat'uNelson Mandela, a clear indication that South Africans were truly on the road to attaining their freedom. The broadcast of President de Klerk's announcement generated a level of excitement such as I had never witnessed before – suddenly, with rapturous spontaneity, as if someone had hit an 'on' switch somewhere. Everyone, the young and the old, were united in celebrating. We all believed that we were truly about to enter 'another country', in the words of the popular band, Mango Groove: a free, democratic, non-racial South Africa. But it was not *uhuru* just yet, and we readied ourselves for the tough task we knew awaited us.

Although I had assisted with the work of the Health Task Team that my husband and so many participated in, especially on the occasions when we set up emergency response health teams at the various rallies held around the greater Pretoria area, it was the work with women in the community that excited me and felt truly rewarding. Our group of women delighted in sharing the wonderful stories of the things we had observed.

I particularly enjoyed the women's recounting of incidents that had taken place during the celebrations. Everyone commented on how – seemingly out of nowhere – there were suddenly ANC flags all over the place. Those who did not have ANC flags to wave were waving UDF flags. Magogo, a member of the Women's League, told me that she had even seen someone brandishing an IOTT (Independent Order of True Templars) flag. The IOTT is an organisation that espouses sobriety, shunning the consumption of alcoholic drinks. It stands out because of the piousness and stoic demeanour of its adherents. The person Magogo was referring to was an esteemed member of the Atteridgeville community, stoic in demeanour as an IOTT leader, who was thus the last person one would expect to see engaging in any public display of jubilation, especially public revelry.

I first met Magogo in 1992 at an area meeting of the ANC Women's League. She showed exceptional leadership skills. I recall that she said that she had been involved extensively with the underground formations of the ANC before the unbanning of the political organisations.

People had assembled at all open spaces and stadia to celebrate, and it seemed that everyone was gripped in ecstasy. Some adults hoisted metal cans on which they drummed with exuberant ferocity. Others blew feverishly on various kinds of whistles whose shrill sounds punctuated the air with piercing resonance. There was generally a cacophony of loud, jubilant noise.

We waited for the promised release of Nelson Mandela on 11 February

1990, and the whole world watched, enthralled, as the first pictures of him, now a stately old man, were broadcast from outside Victor Vester prison. We listened intently to his words:

> Friends, comrades and fellow South Africans. I greet you all in the name of peace, democracy and freedom for all.
>
> I stand here before you not as a prophet but as a humble servant of you, the people. Your tireless and heroic sacrifices have made it possible for me to be here today. I therefore place the remaining years of my life in your hands.
>
> On this day of my release, I extend my sincere and warmest gratitude to the millions of my compatriots and those in every corner of the globe who have campaigned tirelessly for my release.
>
> I send special greetings to the people of Cape Town, this city which has been my home for three decades. Your mass marches and other forms of struggle have served as a constant source of strength to all political prisoners.
>
> I salute the African National Congress. It has fulfilled our every expectation in its role as leader of the great march to freedom.
> I salute our President, Comrade Oliver Tambo, for leading the ANC ,even under the most difficult circumstances.
>
> I salute the rank and file members of the ANC. You have sacrificed life and limb in the pursuit of the noble cause of our struggle.
>
> I salute combatants of Umkhonto we Sizwe, like Solomon Mahlangu and Ashley Kriel, who have paid the ultimate price for the freedom of all South Africans.
>
> I salute the South African Communist Party for its sterling contribution to the struggle for democracy. You have survived 40 years of unrelenting persecution. The memory of great communists like Moses Kotane, Yusuf Dadoo, Bram Fischer and Moses Mabhida will be cherished for generations to come.

I salute General Secretary Joe Slovo, one of our finest patriots. We are heartened by the fact that the alliance between ourselves and the Party remains as strong as it always was.

I salute the United Democratic Front, the National Education Crisis Committee, the South African Youth Congress, the Transvaal and Natal Indian Congresses and COSATU and the many other formations of the Mass Democratic Movement.

I also salute the Black Sash and the National Union of South African Students. We note with pride that you have acted as the conscience of white South Africa. Even during the darkest days in the history of our struggle you held the flag of liberty high. The large-scale mass mobilisation of the past few years is one of the key factors which led to the opening of the final chapter of our struggle.

I extend my greetings to the working class of our country. Your organised strength is the pride of our movement. You remain the most dependable force in the struggle to end exploitation and oppression.

I pay tribute to the many religious communities who carried the campaign for justice forward when the organisations for our people were silenced.

I greet the traditional leaders of our country – many of you continue to walk in the footsteps of great heroes like Hintsa and Sekhukune.

I pay tribute to the endless heroism of youth, you, the young lions. You, the young lions, have energised our entire struggle.

I pay tribute to the mothers and wives and sisters of our nation. You are the rock-hard foundation of our struggle. Apartheid has inflicted more pain on you than on anyone else.

On this occasion, we thank the world community for their great contribution to the anti-apartheid struggle. Without your support our struggle would not have reached this advanced stage. The sacrifice of the frontline states will be remembered by South Africans forever.

My salutations would be incomplete without expressing my deep appreciation for the strength given to me during my long and lonely years in prison by my beloved wife and family. I am convinced that your pain and suffering was far greater than my own.

Before I go any further, I wish to make the point that I intend making only a few preliminary comments at this stage. I will make a more complete statement only after I have had the opportunity to consult with my comrades.

Today, the majority of South Africans, Black and white, recognise that apartheid has no future. It has to be ended by our own decisive mass action in order to build peace and security. The mass campaign of defiance and other actions of our organisation and people can only culminate in the establishment of democracy. The destruction caused by apartheid on our subcontinent is incalculable. The fabric of family life of millions of my people has been shattered. Millions are homeless and unemployed. Our economy lies in ruins and our people are embroiled in political strife. Our resort to the armed struggle in 1960 with the formation of the military wing of the ANC, Umkhonto we Sizwe, was a purely defensive action against the violence of apartheid. The factors which necessitated the armed struggle still exist today. We have no option but to continue. We express the hope that a climate conducive to a negotiated settlement will be created soon so that there may no longer be the need for the armed struggle.

I am a loyal and disciplined member of the African National Congress. I am therefore in full agreement with all of its objectives, strategies and tactics.

The need to unite the people of our country is as important a task now as it always has been. No individual leader is able to take on this enormous task on his own. It is our task as leaders to place our views before our organisation and to allow the democratic structures to decide. On the question of democratic practice, I feel duty-bound to make the point that a leader of the movement is a person who has been democratically elected at a national conference. This is a principle which must be upheld without any exceptions.

Today, I wish to report to you that my talks with the government have been aimed at normalising the political situation in the country. We have not as yet begun discussing the basic demands of the struggle. I wish to stress that I myself have at no time entered into negotiations about the future of our country except to insist on a meeting between the ANC and the government.

Mr de Klerk has gone further than any other Nationalist president in taking real steps to normalise the situation. However, there are further steps as outlined in the Harare Declaration that have to be met before negotiations on the basic demands of our people can begin. I reiterate our call for, inter alia, the immediate ending of the State of Emergency and the freeing of all, and not only some, political prisoners. Only such a normalised situation, which allows for free political activity, can allow us to consult our people in order to obtain a mandate.

The people need to be consulted on who will negotiate and on the content of such negotiations. Negotiations cannot take place above the heads or behind the backs of our people. It is our belief that the future of our country can only be determined by a body which is democratically elected on a non-racial basis. Negotiations on the dismantling of apartheid will have to address the overwhelming demand of our people for a democratic, non-racial and unitary South Africa. There must be an end to white monopoly on political power and a fundamental restructuring of our political and economic systems to ensure that the inequalities of apartheid are addressed and our society thoroughly democratised.

It must be added that Mr de Klerk himself is a man of integrity who is acutely aware of the dangers of a public figure not honouring his undertakings. But as an organisation we base our policy and strategy on the harsh reality we are faced with. And this reality is that we are still suffering under the policy of the Nationalist government.

Our struggle has reached a decisive moment. We call on our people to seize this moment so that the process towards democracy is rapid and uninterrupted. We have waited too long for our freedom. We can no longer wait. Now is the time to intensify the struggle on all fronts. To relax our efforts now would be a mistake which generations to come will not be able to forgive. The sight of freedom looming on the horizon should encourage us to redouble our efforts.

It is only through disciplined mass action that our victory can be assured. We call on our white compatriots to join us in the shaping of a new South Africa. The freedom movement is a political home for you too. We call on the international community to continue the campaign to isolate the apartheid regime. To lift sanctions now would be to run the risk of aborting the process towards the complete eradication of apartheid.

Our march to freedom is irreversible. We must not allow fear to stand in our way. Universal suffrage on a common voters' role in a united democratic and non-racial South Africa is the only way to peace and racial harmony.

In conclusion, I wish to quote my own words during my trial in 1964. They are true today as they were then:

'I have fought against white domination and I have fought against Black domination. I have cherished the ideal of a democratic and free society in which all persons live together in harmony and with equal opportunities. It is an ideal which I hope to live for and to achieve. But if needs be, it is an ideal for which I am prepared to die.'

We felt that he spoke to each one of us and were spurred to work together during these last resolute steps towards freedom. It was no longer 'Freedom in our Lifetime': it was 'Freedom Now'.

It was a time of hope, and it seemed to me, then, that we were invincible. But so much work still had to be done. Among the urgent tasks at hand – one of the most pressing tasks – was the repatriation of the exiles. That became heart-wrenching work. To help us prepare for receiving the returnees and understanding their needs, the Catholic Church enabled several other women and me to attend a workshop in Zambia where we discussed how to address the challenges of repatriation and reintegration. That meeting was attended by many of the women in the ANC women's section – in particular, the leadership of the ANC Women's Desk, with whom we would continue to work after their repatriation into South Africa.

I also participated in a regional women's sector steering committee, which prepared for the transition process in which the internal and external structures would merge. The committee held its weekly meetings on Tuesday evenings at Shell House, the ANC headquarters in Johannesburg. Mrs Winnie Mandela, whose banning order had just been lifted, participated as the head of the merged PWV (Pretoria, Witwatersrand, Vaal) women's entity; I served as treasurer. There was also an administrator who worked for the committee on a full-time basis.

Inevitably, the regime did not take any of that lying down, and a new and vicious wave of violence commenced. The phrase, 'Black on Black violence' emerged and became commonplace. State-sponsored *askaris* were killing people everywhere, including in trains. Mangosuthu (Gatsha) Buthelezi aligned himself with the enemy, and they visited untold horror and havoc everywhere.

In the townships, also, the municipality seemed intent on a confrontation with the community by making community services inaccessible and unaffordable. So, when in response to a further rent hike, the residents of Atteridgeville/Saulsville declared a new boycott under the auspices of the ASRO, the council responded by switching off the lights. Young activists in the township responded with a 'Switch On the Lights Campaign', reinstating the lights by any means possible, including illegally reconnecting them (Operation Switch On). What followed was a brutal reaction by the authorities, resulting in a virtual cat and mouse between the kids and the police, during which Lucky Phatlane was gunned down.

Lucky's mother was devastated. She had just sent him on an errand to buy some household essentials at the shop. Now he was declared dead. She would not take in any food or drink. The family, neighbours and the congregation of her church tried everything to get her to break her fast, but she was inconsolable. The women comrades had, in vain, decided as a last resort to call upon Umama'uWinnie Mandela. Nomzamo heeded the call and came from Johannesburg to mourn with Lucky's mother and family. Winnie's presence and compassion seemed to cut through the fog of deep melancholy to the heart and soul of the grieving mother. I was reminded that Winnie was a social worker and that she had also been honed by loads and loads of experience, herself a mother and sole breadwinner, like Lucky's mother.

We were amazed at Lucky's mother's transformation but did not have very long to take it in because, as we were leaving the house, to our great surprise, a police Hippo was waiting for us. The occupants threw tear gas canisters at us and were shooting randomly. People were ducking and throwing themselves to the ground, even though they were out in the open without any shield available: no trees or walls. It seemed to me that Nomzamo was immune to the teargas fumes, as her voice could be heard advising us to cover our faces as we coughed and cried, our skin burning from the horrible toxic fumes.

Part of our committee's work was to coordinate, at branch level, the activities that were being organised by the local reception committees responsible for the reintegration of the returning exiles into their communities and families. That was important work, but given the other competing priorities at the time, it was not given sufficient attention. The circumstances of the returnees varied. It was also evident that there were differences in the culture of struggle between the returnees and those of us within the internal structures of the Mass Democratic Movement (MDM).

Those differences would impact on the organisation at the local level and also at the level of the FEDTRAW Interim Committee. There was an ugly contestation between those of us who were internal, and thus considered pro-Winnie Mandela, and the external ANC women cadres. That labelling and assigning of assumed positions to us was disconcerting as we were unfamiliar with that 'faction' approach to organisation. Nevertheless, we continued our weekly meetings, which were becoming more and more confrontational and rather demeaning, until eventually, some of us were expelled.

The events at the regional women's level were unsettling; however, we decided at the branch level to disregard the matter and pay more attention to the more pressing local priorities such as voter education and mass mobilisation. There was also the need to assist our people who had been members of the UDF formations, as part of ASRO, with the implications of the disbanding of the UDF, which was an announcement that had been made at the national level.

During that time, the newly formed Atteridgeville ANC Women's Branch prioritised the task of recruiting members and voters for the ANC. Magogo, in particular, threw herself into the task of mobilising on behalf of the organisation. Elderly as she was, she had the strength of a stallion.

All sectors of the community were drawn into the processes of voter education and voter mobilisation, in many forms. Churches, in particular, were in a position to assist by providing venues for the voter education campaigns to be held. However, even at that time, the agents of the apartheid regime and the police proved to be very disruptive.

Nonetheless, the community held firm and continued in earnest with their attempts to hold the government accountable. The Presbyterian church in Atteridgeville, through the efforts of the Late Mrs Rosina Mphahlele, who passed away in 1998, made it possible for the voter education campaign meetings to be held at that church. On one occasion, however, we had hardly started our meeting when a number of apartheid security police barged in. One of them, a big man who looked like he was in charge, demanded to know what we were doing in the church. He was shouting, '*Wat soek hulle hierso, wat doen hulle hierso*? (What do you want here, what are you doing here?).' Rosina stood up and responded, '*Ons bud hierso* (We are praying here.).'

Mrs Mphahlele was quite a formidable figure, and she spoke authoritatively. Encouraged by the impact of her words on the security policeman, the other women were emboldened to ask questions themselves. One lady asked, 'Who are you, *Meneer*?' The man stood there, amazed at having been asked a question by one of us. He stood there for a while without answering, clearly reluctant to give his real name. Then, there on the table, he spotted a lifeline. The man pointed at the flower arrangement and said, '*Ek is roos* (I am rose).' The flowers he was pointing at were roses, but he certainly was an unlikely rose. We made no further comment, and the security police left unceremoniously as we continued with our discussions.

Despite those disruptions, voter education continued, and in Atteridgeville, the ANC clearly had a huge following.

On 27 April 1994, Black South Africans voted for the first time, and they voted in a democratic dispensation. We all voted. Magogo voted, Ma Nkamane voted, I voted, and there was so much joy. Yet, I could not forget: Mitta Ngobeni would have been 20 years old in 1994: she too would have voted, had she lived. Madipholo Masuku would have voted, too, had she been alive. Ma'Nyathi, my mother, missed voting by just two years.

There was so much focus on those elections that I never really considered or had a clue of what would happen thereafter. I do not think that many did. All that was significant and important to us was that we were voting for a free, democratic South Africa. We had great hopes for a great future.

Part 3

After

I Expect More From You

Because my father fought
for you
Instead of spending time with us
he lay on cement floors
behind bars
behind dustbins
under beds
in wardrobes
for you
He forced my mother up and down
from prisons to hospitals to prisons
baby on back
searching for him
because of you
For you
My mother nursed, sold, sewed
worked hard
when he couldn't work for us
because he worked for you

I expect more from you.

Because my uncle disappeared
post-matric
for you
He left his leg in Lusaka
for you
Became a child with a gun
In foreign bushes
for you
His parents worried
for you

So I expect more from you.

Because uMakazi slept on London benches
for you
My aunt was kicked out of school
left home hidden in bakkies
was locked up alone
in dark cells
counting imaginary stars
for you
She lost her love and buried her child
in an unnamed grave
for you
Even when you tried to kill her
she gave herself to you
Even when you abandoned her
across the oceans
she served you
in green and black
fist-high. Proud
for you!

I remember when we first saw your face
my mother sang for you
in long queues
with ID books and *skhaftinas*
she signed for you
gave her voice to you
understood when *utata* said it would take time
with her last cents
she supported you
while he helped you get on your feet

Because you were the dream
they had for us

I expect more than you
who doesn't even remember her name
who doesn't even appreciate
that she still signs for you

years later
neck-high in bond and car instalment
struggling to buy groceries
Even after you took her husband
then tried to hijack his funeral
Even when you rub your theft in her face
she prays for you
gives to you
no longer expects from you

But I expect more from you!
More than a limping uncle
struggling to get your attention
poor veteran still holding on
to dreams conjured up in Lusaka
still believing all those years away from home
will pay off some day!

More than *uMakazi ononyanyayo*
because your taking never stops!
Struggling to pay hospital bills
while you flaunt Blue Label luxuries
in her face
and pretend you don't remember her
behind high walls with tinted windows

I expect more from you!
Because as much as you gave to us
We gave to you!
Always
With our lives
And our limbs
And our children
We gave
For a dream you keep taking
From us
With each cross you take
And all we get are broken promises

Cheap t-shirts
ooChomee on pot-belly stages
We get raped by our fathers
Our homes get broken into
And still your taking never stops!

We have filled your stadia
We have sung your praises
We have devoted our lives to you!

I Expect MORE From You!

— Vangile Gantsho

Magogo died. It hurts me to say that she died a pauper.

Sadly, I was not there when that happened, but I am saddened when I think of her. The words of Vangile Gantsho's poem 'I Expect More of You' remind me of Magogo: 'Even when you abandoned her … she served you, in green and black, fist high. Proud for you.' That was Magogo: Anna Tsotetsi of Sehlogo Street, Atteridgeville. Magogo who loved the ANC and worked for it, every day of her life. I remember a Magogo who stood proud in court, asserting: 'It is I, me, Accused Number 1. It is me, Anna Tsotetsi!'

Magogo was one of those arrested during our women's march from Pretoria to the heart of apartheid's security apparatus. The delegation Gwen Mahlangu and I were with had gone into Wachthuis and handed over our memorandum, which was cordially received. Our central call was for the release of the political prisoners, following the unbanning of political parties and the release of the Rivonia trialists, including Nelson Mandela.

Magogo was with the group of women who had marched to Compol; however, they, unlike us, had met with a different outcome. Their petition had not been received and, instead, they had been beaten up and chased around the streets of Pretoria, some of them taking refuge among the vendors in Strydom Square, hiding among the wares and thus escaping arrest. The others, including Magogo, did not manage to get away and were arrested.

So now, Magogo was in court, responding to the magistrate who was calling out for Accused Number 1 in the case of the women he was presiding over. The courtroom was full. Our sisters from Johannesburg were there to support the women who had been arrested, as our march had been part of a broader national campaign. And there was Magogo, proud, asserting: 'It is I, me, Accused Number 1. It is me, Anna Tsotetsi!'

Later, when the first local government councillors for the ANC were being elected, Magogo and I were among those with the most votes. The two of us, however, were the only two comrades to be dropped from the list to accommodate, we were told, two others who had not made it. There was no explanation for that: we were just told that our names had been removed at the region. I was honoured by the acknowledgement from the local community of the work we were doing. Two women had come first and second on the list for community representatives, so I was not too perturbed by my removal; however, for Magogo, her removal from the list was deeply upsetting.

Becoming a local councillor would have meant that, for the first time, Magogo would be paid for the work she had already been doing in the community, soldiering on even when those who were getting paid were not doing half of what she did. Magogo was saddened, but not only did she continue serving the organisation, but somehow, she became the primary caregiver for a number of orphaned children. She had tried to alert the appropriate authorities about the destitute children to get their needs addressed, but to no avail. So, Magogo, being Magogo, ended up taking those children into her home.

It should have been easy for her to get assistance; after all, she was doing the very work the state should have been doing. But the comrades were so busy and so important that they didn't have time to hear about Magogo and her challenges. Magogo was beginning to learn that freedom did not come with any change in material conditions; and even worse, the basic services that should have been available for the indigent were merely a theoretical concept that did not translate into her life. The promise of a 'better life for all' did not translate into governance and service delivery at the local government level.

On many occasions, things got so bad that there was no food to eat at Sehlogo Street, and the situation of Magogo and her charges was getting desperate. We tried to help, but of course that could not be sufficient. In front of our eyes, freedom was turning Magogo, a once-proud activist and community worker, into a beggar. She was denied the very dignity she had fought for on behalf of others. Magogo was entitled to formal assistance from the municipality and social services, and she tried very hard to access it, doing everything she was told she needed to do, being sent from pillar to post, but receiving no joy. I know that there are many Magogos: the inconvenient people who have become a nuisance to the state. People who expect those they voted for – who promised to serve them – to actually do that. How could they? Forgive my traitorous heart, but it has to be said. It is an ugly sight to see people being demeaned and devalued every day when they have worked so hard. Surely they deserve better.

> We gave to you!
> Always
> With our lives
> And our limbs
> And our children
> We gave
> For a dream you keep taking
> From us
> With each cross you take
> And all we get are broken promises
> **And still your taking never stops!**
> We have filled your stadia
> We have sung your praises
> We have devoted our lives to you!
>
> I Expect MORE From You!

I am saddened by the situation in Bizana, the place of my birth, and by conditions in Mpondoland and throughout the Eastern Cape. Compared to the current situation, the conditions under which I grew up, although difficult at the time, seem idyllic. The town of Bizana, which continues to serve our *lali*, Ndunge, is in an atrocious state. That place is supposed to celebrate Tat'uTambo. It has always been a crucial transit point for people from the surrounding villages, but now the town with its iconic spots, such as Gushede, is in a state of gross disrepair.

The roads seem to be even worse than they were when I was growing up. Driving in from Natal, once you hit the Eastern Cape, you encounter terrible roads with huge potholes. What astounds me, every time we drive to my home from Durban, are the road signs that say 'Potholes ahead for the next 10 kilometres' or 'Potholes ahead for the next 20 kilometres'. Why are people paid to keep putting up those signs instead of fixing the roads where, each year, so many people are killed, as happened so long ago to my brother, Buti'Nyaniso. There clearly is no intention to do anything about it.

The place of my childhood has changed fundamentally and in a terrible way. It is as if the places where we grew up – where we played and learned together and laughed so much together – never existed. That world has vanished – along with the dreams and aspirations of the people who used to inhabit it. Now it remains only in the memories of those of us who still remember, but there are too few of us left.

The open fields in front of the homestead are now overcrowded with shacks, as far as the eye can see. You have to walk through them (*amatshotshombe*) to reach Mama's house. What is left of the fields we once planted is only a small fraction of what used to be – even smaller than the backyard garden of a four-roomed township house. Those fields that MaNyathi fought so hard to keep and which she had cultivated over the years as a means to feed and educate all of us were fields that she and the women of her *ilima* cultivated with pride as they shared the news of the community and their troubles; as each of them worked to feed children and keep the community viable, even as they knew that the children they were raising would be lost to them as soon as they could be registered at the TEBA offices, in the case of the boys, or find employment in the households in the cities, in the case of the girls.

Those were difficult times, and those women, oMaNyathi and her peers, had built home space and community for us, despite the efforts of the Transkei government. During the time of the Transkei government, there were terrible laws that were applied to our rural communities. For instance, homes were moved and crowded into small spaces. People were made to build their huts on top of graves. There was also the culling of cattle where people were forced to reduce their herds in the name of preventing soil erosion. There had been no research done to see if that could work.

People became poorer and poorer, and democracy exacerbated the situation. There was no attempt to hear from the people or understand their needs. There was no interest in knowing what they thought should be done to heal the land that had sustained them over the years and strengthen the communities that had survived, despite many decades, even centuries, of abuse.

Instead, the offspring of Ndunge and other rural communities were given whatever small amounts those in government thought constituted sufficient reimbursement for their disenfranchisement and all that had been stolen from them throughout the apartheid years. It seems that the so-called traditional leaders participated in that outcome. The same traditional leaders who had colluded with the apartheid regime now seek to continue their despotic rule – this time, in collusion with the democratic government. Now, it is the representatives of the 'democratic ANC government' who meet with the headmen at the various Great Places, and the people living in the rural areas are simply subjected to whatever they decree. The poor people accept whatever they are given because, no matter how small it is, it is better than nothing. It is ironic that people who successfully resisted disenfranchisement by the apartheid regime are now being subjugated by a democratic government.

We have a government that we and our families have suffered and died to bring into existence. But in my experience, our people have never been more disempowered and vulnerable than they are now. We are being ruled, but no one takes the responsibility to govern, to lead, and no one can be held accountable for anything. Whenever one has to seek assistance from the government, one must first confront a disinterested civil servant. That civil 'servant', the face and voice of our democratic government, will tell you: 'I am not responsible for that' or 'I will come back to you as soon as possible'. Unfortunately, it never becomes possible. One is effectively dismissed from their presence and nothing ever gets done.

So it seems that that is what transpired in the case of the land in Ndunge. Some important people decided to facilitate the creation of densified squatter communities on land that had been used for subsistence farming while not providing alternative forms of livelihood, which effectively turned those communities into people dependent on social grants and remittances from family and relatives living or working in the urban areas.

↭

Later, around 2002, when I was in Malaysia where my husband was the South African High Commissioner, I received the news that the land had been cut up and I was due the sum of R8,000. No other information. I tried to understand the basis for the apportioning of the land and the resultant 'remuneration', but I never got any explanation at all, only the shock when I went home and saw what had been done.

Then, out of nowhere, years later, I received a communication from the provincial government in the Eastern Cape advising me to report to East London to receive the remainder of what was allegedly due to me. I responded by calling the official there, a Mr Tau Leeu, thanking him for the communication and asking him for advice as to the nature of the allocation I was supposed to receive. He told me that he was not in a position to provide details about the said allocation, except that they had made arrangements for me to receive it at their offices in East London. I suggested that, as I had no idea what I would be travelling for, it would be best if he facilitated for whatever allocation they were talking about to be directed to me in Pretoria, where I lived. I informed him that a return trip to East London would cost me more than the first allocation they had sent me.

After consulting with his superiors, Mr Leeu returned to say that that could be done. However, I was to send an affidavit (certified by a commissioner of oaths), a certified copy of my ID and my bank details to enable him to do it. I was uncomfortable but sent the details, as requested, via DHL.

I waited a long time; then I decided to call and enquire. Mr Leeu claimed that he had never received the communication, so I tracked it with DHL and was told by a receptionist that a notification had been received at their offices but no one had fetched the documents and, somehow, they no longer had the notification – or the time had expired. Whatever it was, they did not have my communication. The long and the short of it is that I was asked to send the above-mentioned personal details to the offices of the provincial government for the second time, at my own expense. So I did, again; and again, there was no response from the provincial government, no acknowledgement of receipt, no knowledge of the tracking number. No joy.

After a lot of to-ing and fro-ing, I resorted to the Public Protector's office where I was directed to another official who requested the same information and would also not divulge the nature of the allocation. He asked that I write to him with the details I had, which I did, and that was the end of the road. I became too exhausted to bother, which, I am sure, must have been the intention in the first place. It saddens me when I recall how Mama had fought for that land and her triumph all those years ago.

༄

After 1992, as we joined the ANC-led Post-Apartheid South Africa initiative, I travelled to Lusaka to attend a workshop on the policy framework for care institutions in the country, post-apartheid, which was hosted by Mama Njobe, Head of the Women's Section of the ANC. I loved the women of the ANC I met on that occasion, but I was a bit uncomfortable, although at the time it was difficult to give voice to the exact reason for that. The women there clearly cared a lot, from a welfare perspective, about the well-being of people in institutions. Lilian Ngoyi, a pioneer of the women's movement in South Africa and co-founder of the Federation of South African Women, had been famously passionate about institutions for the care of the vulnerable, and she always made a point of visiting such places whenever she travelled outside of South Africa. Lilian was particularly impressed with the institutions she saw in the socialist countries, and I understood why.

In honour of her, the ANC Women's Section took on the cause, and addressing the social needs of the people, including care for the vulnerable and frail, became their responsibility. However, as champions of that initiative, they did not mainstream it into the broader policy work of the ANC. That work was not a natural fit for the ANC Women's Section, so by taking it on, they essentially marginalised it.

I would have ample time to reflect upon that and try to understand some of the dynamics at play when, in 1995, I travelled to England where I had registered at the Centre for International Child Health at the University of London for an M.Phil. in Community-Based Rehabilitation of People with Disabilities. I had decided to take a sabbatical to allow myself time to think more clearly about the issues of the needs of children with disabilities in South Africa.

Although a lot of that work did not find resonance within the ANC policy debates, I was aware of a growing number of professional women who were taking it on and helping to broaden the discussion – women such as Rosina Mphahlele in Atteridgeville and Mosima Francesca Sethosa in Mamelodi, to name just two. What was frustrating is that the Department of Education ignored their expertise only to draw them out when a public statement had to be made – all to create the impression that the matter was receiving adequate attention from policymakers.

When I arrived in London, it was to join a diverse group of people from countries in West Africa, South America and Asia. All of them had extensive experience in the management and care of people with disabilities and all offered an insight into their countries and their approach to that issue. Most of us from the Global South held a strong view that one of the biggest problems faced by our countries was the lack of institutions dedicated to the care of children with disabilities. We had heard accounts of how that left the responsibility of looking after those children to women who were burdened with other responsibilities and had no significant support or assistance. We learnt that those from the Global North had problems similar to ours and had some that were more peculiar. For instance, in England, Margaret Thatcher had famously closed the majority of care institutions with the result that many people with mental disabilities were left to wander the streets aimlessly.

There were consequently few if any dedicated functional publicly funded care facilities left in the United Kingdom, and special needs children were increasingly being left in the care of family members (most often, their mothers). That was not a new experience for the women in those communities. Previously, the problem had been that the care facilities for children with special needs were concentrated in the more affluent areas and were not accessible to them. The poor and marginalised immigrant communities had therefore evolved their own solutions and were not affected by the Thatcher intervention, which would change the face and character of institutionalisation in the UK.

Since most of us who were registered with the Centre for International Child Health were interested in understanding how the community-based rehabilitation of people with disabilities was being managed in England, we appreciated the opportunity our course afforded us to visit some of the most impoverished communities there and view, first-hand, some of the solutions those communities utilised.

During my research, I had focused my work on two groups of parents and caregivers of children with special needs at the Tower Hamlets Borough, one of the most impoverished areas in the United Kingdom. I thought that, although the context was different, in many ways, the conditions those people faced were similar to those encountered by the communities I had worked with at home. The one group consisted of members of the Bangladeshi community, and the other was comprised of multiracial parents of people with special needs. I had documented the voices of those caregivers in my thesis. The most important lesson that I learned during my stay in

England was that the parents of children with special needs themselves need special care. In that respect, I saw how they appreciated one another as part of a vital support system, as they often felt isolated from society.

We found some innovative community strategies in those poor, culturally diverse communities. What had the most impact on me was how the women pooled together to provide care for the children. That was stimulating for the little ones who played and learned together. While some of the mothers looked after the children, others went to work. Those who worked contributed to the upkeep of the childcare centre and a stipend for the childcare mothers. A parents' committee managed the school, raised funds and created a relationship with the local municipality who provided input through professionals who would assist the parents. The most significant benefit, though, was the opportunity for the parents to learn skills and gain certification while looking after the children. Later on, they could branch off and find better-paying employment and contribute financially to the running of the school. That thrilled me, and I could not wait to go home and share details about it with the caregivers and parents of special needs children with whom I worked at Medicos.

And so it was. When I got home, I shared what I had learnt with the Medicos caregivers and parents. As I expected, they were enthralled and insisted that we start a similar initiative in South Africa. Immediately, all of the Medicos caregivers wanted to participate. As mentioned, they were all grandparents, mostly *gogos* and one grandfather. The caregivers enthusiastically established a schedule of weekly meetings during which they would discuss their issues and the new initiative, which was named Tirisano. Soon, chapters of the Tirisano Networks began springing up everywhere.

Tirisano had two components. The first was for the parents and caregivers and was vital to the overall programme. We modelled it on the English case study from my research. The caregivers and parents were given skills training and the means for income generation. They started with sewing lessons and were soon producing merchandise such as school uniforms and, later, bedding, for which they received commissions from the local schools they supplied. The revenue was divided among the caregivers with the remainder reinvested into the project for future materials. The second component was the care of children with special needs. After school, they were looked after and helped with skills development, which was especially important for those youth over 18 years of age.

There were challenges, of course, which we started discussing at the first annual general meeting of the Tirisano Networks where the organisation was officially launched. I was appointed as Chair, and Mrs Sangweni was elected as Treasurer. It was my responsibility to invite Mrs Zanele Mbeki and Yvonne Chaka Chaka to be patrons of the organisation.

We had several offers of assistance. Mrs Ngele, mayor of Pretoria, facilitated a donation of top-quality sewing machines from the spouses of members of the diplomatic corps stationed in Pretoria. We had identified a place from which our initiative could operate: the erstwhile Putco Bus land outside of Atteridgeville, near the hospital. It was ideal for our needs, and the municipality awarded it to us. But we could never take occupation of it because, when we got there, we found that a man had moved in. He told us that if we intended to use the property, we would first have to remove his dead body from it. When we informed the municipality about what had happened, they told us that we could use their offices until they sorted out the squatter. As far as they were concerned, that was the end of the issue. We never occupied that land.

We continued with the sewing lessons and production of uniforms at the municipal offices and held the caregiver meetings at the Medicos Special School. We struggled on, focusing on strengthening the relationships between the caregivers while learning about the challenges that confronted them. The biggest of those was that once a special needs child turned 18, they had to leave the care institution and were often left at home with no hope of employment. We wondered if we could explore working relationships with existing industries to become centres of production for selected items. We wanted to provide opportunities for the children and youth. We also wanted them and their caregivers to be able to visit such places as Robben Island and see Mandela's prison cell. All involved had so many dreams and believed that they could make them happen.

In 1999, my husband Abe, who then was a Member of Parliament and Chair of the Parliamentary Portfolio Committee on Health, was awarded the Nelson Mandela Award for Health and Human Rights by The Henry J. Kaiser Foundation. He donated that award to Tirisano.

That translated into a lot of goodwill, and the idea was so attractive to development partners that they wanted to help us build the premises of Tirisano as envisaged in our business plan. But there was no movement in that regard, which was frustrating. People just ignored our pleas and appeals while making it clear that we were annoying them and that they were in charge. It was evident that children with disabilities and their care fell under the radar of their concerns. We soldiered on, nevertheless, and Tirisano continued to grow.

Then, in 2002, when Abe was appointed as South Africa's High Commissioner to Malaysia, we decided that I should join him for that posting, which meant that I had to leave my employment at the Department of Health and my community programmes, including the Tirisano Networks and PEPPs (Project for the Establishment of Pre-primary Schools), an initiative I had started with some others.

As soon as I left, Tirisano changed track. The person appointed to run the day-to-day work of the organisation was the lady in charge of the income generation programmes who, as it turned out, had neither the interest nor the inclination to proceed with the core functions of the organisation. It was not long before the other board members were edged out and Mrs Sangweni resigned as treasurer. Her major gripe being that, without the knowledge of the board members, the contact details of the organisation had been changed, and all mail, including the financials, were being redirected to a postal address that they were not privy to. In addition, the organisation was no longer in compliance with the requirements of the Department of Social Development for registered non-profit organisations (NPOs), as it continued to receive donations and grants meant for the development of initiatives such as those mentioned above and to address the needs of parents of children with disabilities. In my absence, however, Tirisano was misused and had started operating as an income-generating venture.

My efforts to communicate were ignored, so I contacted the Department of Social Development to inform them of the situation that had arisen at Tirisano. At first, the directorate responsible for NPOs seemed understanding. They told me that what had happened was criminal and that they were going to address the situation. After several failed attempts to meet with the people who were trading as Tirisano, Mr Bok Mapena, initially the director and then chief director of the NPO division at the Department of Social Development, scheduled a meeting in Atteridgeville, where he said he would go to the police station to institute charges against the people involved. But Mr Bok was a no-show, and we found ourselves chasing after him.

Bok never met with us again after that, and soon there was a new Minister of Social Development and a new Acting Director General. We attended more meetings to introduce the subject; more promises were made that something would be done, and then silence – again. We never received responses to our communications. I gave up.

Years later, when we had returned after completing our tours of duty in Malaysia (2002–2006) and then Canada (2006–2010), where Abe had also been stationed as High Commissioner, I was surprised when two women I did not know came to see me at our home. It was known that I had returned and would most likely be seeking answers about Tirisano. During my absence, the enterprise had been dissolved and its assets distributed among the women who worked there. Those two were upset because they had only received R6,000 each and felt that they had been cheated. Once again, I approached the Department of Social Development and, receiving no joy, decided to go to the Office of the Public Protector. They told me that I had to provide them with Tirisano annual reports and asked that I kindly comply. It was clear that there was no point in proceeding further. It would have been kinder to tell me straight out that they had no interest in pursuing the matter.

Also, while we were away on mission in Malaysia, my husband's practice in Saulsville, Number 42 Loetse Street, was hijacked and occupied under very odd circumstances by a woman who ran a 'creche'. All of our attempts to rectify the situation were fruitless, and so the situation remained until 2019. We went to every office, from the various officials of local government to the Minister of Social Development at the time, Minister Edna Molewa, who was very gracious – to no avail. We explained that the neighbours had approached us in frustration, complaining of unsanitary conditions. The facility housing the preschool children operated without a sewerage system and, instead, buckets were used for that purpose and the contents disposed of out in the open, daily. The local councillors, it later transpired, were renting out the property to the lady who was running the creche, which frustrated any effort to remove her. She insisted that she would not move, and we eventually gave up, having exhausted every avenue with no joy.

Eventually, an old gentleman from our community who had also been involved in a battle to reclaim his family property, which had been stolen by the local government councillors in a similar fashion to ours, came to see us at our house. He reported that after battling away with no results, he was directed to the municipal offices in the Pretoria CBD, and there, he had finally received help. After finalising his matter, he was speaking with the young ladies who had assisted him about the scope of the problem of thievery by the municipal officials in Atteridgeville and the wider Pretoria region. During their discussion, the young ladies asked him if he knew Dr Nkomo. When he answered in the affirmative, they asked him if he knew that he had died. The man was appalled by that question and said that as far as he was aware, Dr Nkomo was very much alive. The officials who were helping him were astonished. They had been instructed to sign over the number 42 Loetse property to the occupant, as they had been informed that my husband had died. So this gentleman had come to tell us to get to the Madiba Street municipal offices so the officials could confirm that my husband was alive and not proceed with the transaction they had been advised to conclude, given his, I guess, fortunate demise.

Following that, my husband and daughter went to the Tshwane Municipality offices to confirm that the news of his death was untrue. I am told that the lady who had asked for my husband to come to the office, Ms Mabel Booysen, was shocked to see him in living flesh. She works in an open-plan office, and I am told that many of her colleagues congregated around them to see the apparition who had descended there.

We are also dealing with another instance of grand theft by Tshwane municipal officials: *Doda's* land in Winterveldt, which he left to Abe and his family. That land has also been stolen. Again, we tried everything, but the mayor's comment to my husband was: 'But you know that our officials are thugs and thieves.' He promised to deal with the matter, but to no avail. We are now engaged in lengthy legal processes, at great expense, to reclaim Dr W. F. Nkomo's property, the theft of which was facilitated by an ANC councillor based at the municipal offices of the ANC government who continue to undermine justice.

꒷

I have always invisaged a 'Free South Africa' as a place where one has a strong government that governs in the interests of the people. 'The people shall govern' had always been our rallying call. And we entrusted our organisation, the African National Congress, with that task. But instead of the better life for all that we had invisaged and been promised, we found ourselves again stripped of our agency and ruled and subjected to tyranny and total disregard.

During the first five years of freedom, we truly believed that we had started on a journey towards achiving *uhuru*. The South African Constitution was enacted with its Bill of Rights, as were the many laws aimed at eradicating apartheid and the effects of its practices.

In terms of the South African Constitution, education is a right that every child should be granted; yet, so much prevents children from accessing it. And it is criminal that the poor continue to be denied access to the most basic amenities, which can result in the attempt to access education literally becoming a deadly undertaking. As it was for Michael Konopi, who drowned in faeces in a pit-latrine, 70 years after I left Ndunge Primary School.

There is no governance. The country is left on auto-pilot, and those we have entrusted with the task of governing display their irritation when their attention is directed towards the work to be done – the work for which they are handsomely remunerated to perform. I have been dismissed so many times for doing that, probably because I dare to expect people to leave the more lucrative exercise of looking out for looting opportunities and do the work they are being paid to do.

I have learnt a lot in my lifetime – many lessons, and the saddest of them is that we are living in a time of widespread impunity. A time when children still have to learn under trees and use pit latrines.